PRAISE FOR *THE TIME CLEANSE*

"Your greatest returns on happiness, growth, and success come from optimizing your most valuable resource: TIME. Griffith shows you how."
—SHAWN ACHOR
New York Times bestselling author of
The Happiness Advantage and *Big Potential*

"Mastering your reality includes the ability to master your time. In *The Time Cleanse*, Steven shows you how to mindfully master your precious time for what matters most both personally and professionally."
—ISAAC LIDSKY
New York Times bestselling author of *Eyes Wide Open*

"In an age where time can be the greatest barrier to your success, Steven's Time Cleanse process shows you how to take control of your time and regain valuable hours to get fit, healthy, and realize your full potential in all areas of your life."
—MARK MACDONALD
New York Times bestselling author of *Body Confidence*

"Steven teaches us in a very pragmatic and insightful way how to perform with our time so that we can do more, get more, and be more. He inspires us to rise to perhaps our greatest calling—investing in mastering our time. Well done."
—J.D. MEIER
author of *Getting Results the Agile Way*

"Steven has laid out *the* successful theory of our human relationship with time—impressively revolutionary to our old thinking as quantum mechanics is to old Newtonian physics. When applied, *The Time Cleanse* radically upgrades our perception of the 'limits' of personal productivity and performance. Read it and see for yourself."
—THOM KNOLES
Maharishi (master) of Vedic meditation

THE
TIME
CLEANSE

A PROVEN SYSTEM TO ELIMINATE WASTED TIME,

REALIZE YOUR FULL POTENTIAL,

AND REINVEST IN WHAT MATTERS MOST

STEVEN GRIFFITH

New York   Chicago   San Francisco   Athens
London   Madrid   Mexico City   Milan
New Delhi   Singapore   Sydney   Toronto

1 2 3 4 5 6 7 8 9   QVS   24 23 22 21 20 19

ISBN   978-1-260-14309-6
MHID   1-260-14309-0

e-ISBN   978-1-260-14310-2
e-MHID   1-260-14310-4

Library of Congress Cataloging-in-Publication Data

Names: Griffith, Steven, author.
Title: The time cleanse : a proven system to eliminate wasted time, realize
  your full potential, and reinvest in what matters most / Steven Griffith.
Description: New York : McGraw-Hill, [2019]
Identifiers: LCCN 2018053660 | ISBN 9781260143096 (alk. paper) | ISBN
  1260143090
Subjects: LCSH: Time management.
Classification: LCC BF637.T5 G75 2019 | DDC 650.1/1—dc23
LC record available at https://lccn.loc.gov/2018053660

McGraw-Hill Education books are available at special quantity discounts to use as premiums and sales promotions or for use in corporate training programs. To contact a representative, please visit the Contact Us pages at www.mhprofessional.com.

It's your time

Contents

PART I   PREPARE

In Part I, I will prepare you for the Time Cleanse process; I'll take you through how time works in today's modern age; help you shift your relationship with time in a way that supports you; get you clear on what's truly important to you; and show you how to identify the toxins that are stopping you from achieving what you want.

PART II   PROCESS

In Part II, I'll take you through the Time Cleanse process for both your life and your business, help you reclaim lost time, and I'll show you how to reinvest your reclaimed time in what matters most to you for optimal results.

PART III   PERFORM

In Part III, I'll show you with your new relationship with time how to improve the quality, experience, and performance with your time; how to identify what your personal "Time Type" is; as well as increase your productivity with cutting-edge tools, tips, and tactics.

Acknowledgments

A SAYING I'VE USED FOR MANY YEARS IS "YOU ALWAYS do it yourself, but you never do it alone." This Acknowledgment shows so clearly how true this is. I want to first acknowledge all the coaches and mentors who have contributed to and helped me on my journey these many years without whom none of this would be possible. To the thousands of clients and students I have been honored to work with, I've learned so much from you and what the human spirit is capable of. So many people over the years have helped me, and if I have not included you in these acknowledgments, that was not my intention.

Thank you, Mom, for the many sacrifices you made along the way for me and for teaching me what grit is all about. Thank you to my friend, mentor and boxing coach, Tom Delaney, for your kindness, compassion, generosity, and love—for believing in me, always being in my corner, and demonstrating what a "coach" really is. I carry that with me every day. Yuki Shinozaki, your deep love and support helped bring this vision into the world from the very start. You inspired me and motivated me in so many ways—I couldn't have done it without you.

My agent, Greg Ray, thank you for believing in me and this book and for your guidance and support each step of the way in helping me bring *The Time Cleanse* to the world—massive gratitude. Cheryl Ringer, my editor at McGraw-Hill: I knew after our first meeting that you saw the vision, and I was right. Thanks for your brilliant editing and guidance on making this book. You're amazing! David Christel, thank you for the many years of friendship, continual support, love, and hours of laughter. Your contribution to this book in editing, making suggestions, and organizing was so graciously provided when it was needed most. Nancy Hancock, the Google of books: Thank you for all your wisdom and guidance as well as the many hours of discussions to help me craft this book and deliver my message.

To Mark Macdonald, the best nutritionist on the planet, thank you for your friendship, motivation, and guidance all these years and especially for helping me make this book possible. Your nutrition wisdom and education have kept me healthy and fueled to keep moving forward delivering my message—big hugs to you. Ryan Brown, thank you for your friendship, contribution, and insights to this book. You were always there for whatever I needed. And thank you, Rivka, for helping craft the many stories for this book and your constant support, guidance, and words of encouragement. You're an amazing storyteller.

Pat Allen, your guiding principles have helped shape my life as a man and as a coach. Thank you for your loving spirit, support, and encouragement of my work all these years. Geoffry White, thank you for your friendship and advice in the good times and challenging ones. You truly have been in my corner all the way. Thank you, Thom Knoles, for your wisdom, guidance, and meditation instruction and for always telling how it is with such elegance—you always know the right thing to say.

Charles Pence, it has been an honor to coach you these many years and watch you compress time. You are one of the rare individuals who keeps pushing forward no matter what. Pat Norton, I am grateful for your ongoing friendship, backing, and the many laughs we've had together. Thank you for the trust you put in me to coach you; it is awesome to watch you transform your life and the lives of the people you touch. Alex Ochart, thank you for your enthusiasm, creative input, and motivation when this all started—you helped me get the ball rolling. Jim Hjort, thanks for your friendship, encouragement, review of my manuscript, and all the great laughs. Keith Koons, thank you for your insights, writing, and the help you gave me in getting my ideas on paper.

Thank you, John Dewey, for your always being there in friendship and support, your kind words that helped keep me pushing forward, and our long talks that continually inspired me and your behind-the-scenes contribution to helping me get this message out to the world. John Morrow: from the early days at SOP's, you've always been there for me in friendship and support. Thank you, my friend.

To my friends Kristie, George, and Sophia Kosmides, your constant love and support kept me buoyed and on course. Kristie: You have been there from the very beginning when I wrote my very first book in Hawaii, always supporting me with your love and friendship—I truly appreciate it. Thank you. George: I wrote every day with your picture on my desk to remind me of the hope you boldly stood for and lived by every day. You helped so many people—you are truly missed, my friend.

My brother, Matt, thank you for your support and friendship as we grow older as brothers. David Sullivan: You helped me in the early days land my first corporate client. I will always remember that and am grateful for your friendship and constant encouragement. Allen Hoey, since our days at the gym, you always have had such sage wisdom for me. I appreciate your friendship and support these many years. Chris Harvey, your creative influence, your masterful photography, your friendship, and our deep conversations have always served to inspire me. Mindy Mai, for your support, patience, love, and endless food deliveries—thank you so much. Misha and Denise Georgevitch, thank you for all the love and support you've given me and great home-cooked meals. Liam Roberts, thanks for all the talks on our early-morning paddleboarding trips as I worked to complete this book—your support is truly appreciated. To Gary De Rodriguez: You started me on the path so many years ago, helping me to see who I truly am and what I am capable of. Thank you. Marilyn Youngbird, thank you for your powerful medicine and guidance during my first vision quest that helped me clear the way to discover my true purpose. James Malinchak, for your inspiring support and encouragement to write books—big thanks. C.J. Matthews, thank you for your ongoing friendship, always believing in me, and supporting me in the good times and bad.

Charmain Page, thank you for your love, wisdom, and firm push every time I needed it. Gay Hendricks: Your writing inspired me and my work. Vaughan Risher, thank you for your creative thinking, filming, and website design and support. Nancy Njdeyo, thank you for your research for this book. Wayne Dyer, your work allowed me to look at the world with new possibilities. Bryan Tracy, thank you for the wisdom and insights from all your books. Jon Kabat-Zinn, thank you for your mindfulness, your wisdom, and your early writing that got me on the path of mindfulness. Doug DeLuca, I am grateful for your friendship, encouragement, and support of my career. Thank you, Terese Mulvihill, for your friendship and always supportive talks. And thank you to the staff at the Villas-Santosh, Kealoha, and Chuck, and Matt: You guys helped create the best environment for me to work in and write this book.

Pete Zachary, thank you for trusting in me to guide you to reclaim your time and for contributing your story to the book. Natalie Collins, thank you for being an amazing host to my weekly Monday Morning Motivation podcast. Kentay Williams, I am grateful for your assistance and for helping me launch my first Time Cleanse event. And Peter Hyoguchi, I am grateful for your filming and creative input. Vi Rooks for your meditation guidance and support. Liz Fiori, thank you for helping me stay healthy. Thank you, Bibi Goldstein, for you and your team's support behind the scenes. Linda Buffington, thank you for your great event support. Mark Kendrick for your legal support. Shianne Gobin for all your help. Paul Zehrer for your support. Thank you to Adam Miller, Ann Hamilton, Grant Heller, Norm and Debbie Compton, Mike Hibner, Lisa Pantastico, and Chris Campbell for being in the group of original Time Cleansers and being fearless in reclaiming your time. Thank you Taita Juan Guillermo Chindoy, Carlos Duran, Alejandra DeLuca, Liz Bowlus, and staff for your amazing support on my journey. Neil Strauss, thank you for your support and trust in me to work with your powerful syndicate. Sandy and Doug McMaster, for your beautiful Hawaiian slack key music that I listened to for hours as I wrote. *Mahalo.*

Introduction

IT'S YOUR TIME . . .

Time is your most valuable, precious, and limited resource; yet we make the mistake of throwing it away, not protecting it, and allowing it to be stolen from us all the time because we believe it's unlimited. It's not. Your time is actually limited. In fact, it is the one resource that you can't get back once it's gone.

Time is the great equalizer. Each and every one of us has exactly 24 hours, or 1,440 minutes, in a day. We were born on an exact date at an exact time, and then we leave life with an equally precise time stamp. That time is your *life*.

The quality of your life is determined by how you choose to use your time (or how time uses you). You have a specific relationship with time because everyone's time relationship is unique.

What is your relationship with time? Is it serving you? Is it an abundant environment within you? Or does it seem like it controls you and prevents you from feeling like you're never able to relax, be yourself, or express your full potential?

By the end of this book, you will see that this is your most important relationship, and you will learn if time is either serving you or enslaving you.

For over 25 years I've been driving high performance and unlocking potential in top executives, CEOs, entrepreneurs, military leaders, pro athletes, and celebrities. These are the truly elite and incredibly successful professionals that have achieved amazing things in their careers. I don't say this to impress you. I say this because it's important to note that these incredibly successful people were all hardworking and full of motivation, but they all had one problem in common—they all needed more time and freedom in their schedules and in their lives.

About five years ago I had a realization. All my clients were being held back by the same roadblock. They even used the exact same statement to describe it: "I just don't have enough time." Even with all their success, they still wanted and needed more time.

I would talk to corporate executives that didn't have enough time to go to their son's or daughter's sports game. There were business owners who hadn't taken a vacation in years. So many of my clients felt rushed, stressed, overwhelmed, and constantly distracted. It was the number one topic of every coaching session and corporate engagement.

I saw the toll it was taking on these good people. From damaged careers, financial struggles, and unhappy families, to poor health, fatigue and stress, my clients were constantly struggling to live their best lives.

They were missing life while living it. They were living like victims of time.

After realizing how serious this was, I committed to figuring out this universal issue: *How do we get more time back in our lives and be more productive with the time we have, so we can do the things we truly care about and that matter the most?*

I traveled the world researching and studying everything I could get my hands on to find the solution and crack this code. I wanted to figure out a way to be more effective, efficient, and productive in modern life.

My journey took me from the modern laboratories of the leading neuroscientists and mathematicians, to the ancient wisdom of Buddhist monks in Thailand and Japan. I learned from the top mindfulness and performance psychology researchers and even from some of Einstein's theories on how to unlock more time.

What I found shocked me.

I ultimately uncovered a series of steps and actions that accelerated people's ability to recognize the barriers in their beliefs, behaviors, and mental and emotional patterns that were keeping them from having important breakthroughs with their time. And now, all that I learned, discovered, developed, and taught to thousands of people is finally here in the pages of this book, *The Time Cleanse*.

By embracing and applying the principles laid out in this book, *get up to 20 hours a week or more of your free time as a result*. Simultaneously, you'll squeeze every drop of productivity and performance out of every hour, so you'll always have time available for the things that matter most in business and in life. And I know this because it has worked for me and each and every client.

The Time Cleanse is a process that shows you how to *do more, get more, and be more* by eliminating the time toxins and contaminants that have been stealing your time, energy, and focus, so you can live a happier, more fulfilling life, where the pressure of time no longer has a hold on you.

You might be saying to yourself, "That sounds great but . . ."

1. "I'm already working at maximum capacity."

2. "How do I increase productivity?"

3. "How is it possible to take time off?"

4. "How do I deal with distractions?"

5. "I've already tried the best time management systems."

6. "Where do I get the energy to do it all?"

I made all those excuses, too, until I discovered that I was using old, outdated time management techniques that no longer apply and are not relevant in the twenty-first century.

Don't worry. I promise we'll address all of this and more. *The Time Cleanse* offers a new approach that will help you accelerate your progress toward any dream or desire you want and are seeking.

Until now, the most common advice given to be successful is you must "work harder," "hustle more," or "grind it out!" But you can only do this for so long. This is not sustainable, and grinding doesn't help you deal with the source of the problem: the feeling that you don't have enough time! *The Time Cleanse* is here to change these overplayed mantras and beliefs. This book will teach you that it's not about time management; it's about understanding and mastering your performance with time. You see, in traditional time management, time is considered a scarce resource that is always ticking away. You're always "on the clock," which creates an intense *time* pressure and a need to get a lot done in every minute. This makes time an adversary that you are battling against.

That kind of thinking does not create a peaceful mental state or help you perform at your highest level. Plus, most of us can't stay organized enough to "manage" our time every hour of every day. That's just not how real life works.

Think about your closest relationships: your mom, dad, sister, brother, wife, husband, best friend, children, or grandchildren. Is your goal to manage them? Of course not! You can't "manage" your intimate relationships. You have to work at and flow with them. Your goal with time should be the same. Not to control it, but be an ally, partner, or teammate through the good times and the bad. Time can be your ultimate supporter and ally, but only if you have the right relationship with it.

Fortunately, there is a path to freedom. But it's not what you think. We live in a world not only where things are designed to steal our time, interrupt us, and take us off course, but where our brains are being programmed to desire constant distraction, taking us farther away from our original purpose and intention. You cannot "manage" these kinds of distractions and activities—time management doesn't work in the twenty-first century.

You need new thinking and a new approach! That's a bold statement for a book about time, but it's something I've had to come to grips with in my own life and in the lives of my super-performing clients.

The Time Cleanse is a time performance system that will teach you how to use your time as it was meant to be used once and for all—to get what you really want in business and in life, as quickly as possible, while having fun doing it.

You may even find yourself sharing the same amazing results as the stories you'll read about in the next chapters, including:

- A real estate pro who condensed an entire year's worth of productivity into a single quarter . . . then went on to break his all-time annual sales record!

- A CEO who reclaimed one whole day per week to spend with his daughter.

- An executive who started his own consulting firm from his reclaimed time and achieved his lifelong dream of being his own boss.

By the end of this book, not only will you perform better, but you will be able to bend time to your will and literally "create time."

Developing the Time Cleanse and thinking about time in a whole new way has changed everything for me and my clients. Some of them made more money, quit their jobs to pursue their dreams, started businesses; others finished writing books they'd always wanted to publish, some even started nonprofits to help others, and many finally made the big decision to focus more on what was most important to them: their families and loved ones. No matter the specifics, all of them performed better, while feeling more successful, happy, and fulfilled in their lives. They were cleansed. Time toxins were no longer hijacking their energy, focus, and dreams.

HOW TO GET THE MOST OUT OF THIS BOOK

I realize that your time is your most valuable asset, and as the author of this book, I want you to get the maximum return on your time. That's my commitment to you. There are many things you can be doing with your time and you chose this book. I'm grateful for the trust you've given me, which I don't take lightly.

My promise to you is for you to get back a minimum of 10 hours per week, which thousands of people have done using the Time Cleanse system with most of them getting up to 20 hours or more back. This is not a made-up number. It's what I've seen repeatedly with my corporate, individual, and live-event clients. With getting back just 10 hours a week, that's 40 hours a month, 480 hours a year.

The Time Cleanse is presented in three sections.

- **PART I "PREPARE"** In this section, I will prepare you for the cleanse. I'll take you through what time is really for and how it works. I'll show you how to overcome the effects of time pressure and how to shift your relationship with time, and I'll prove to you that there is an abundance of time. You will learn why traditional time management techniques no longer work in today's modern technology-driven world. You'll discover what is contaminating your time and learn how to break through the blind spots that keep you feeling stuck. I'll help you get clear on your goals and purpose and show you how to set your intentions to increase your chances of success.

- **PART II "PROCESS"** In this section, I'll take you through the Time Cleanse process for both your life and your business, helping you reclaim your time, and then show you how to reinvest your reclaimed time for what matters most to you in your business and life. You'll learn the process for getting your best Return on Time (ROT) going forward for the biggest results.

- **PART III "PERFORM"** In the final section of the book, I will show you how to have a new relationship with time that supports you—improving your quality, experience, and performance with time—and how to set up your perfect day to perform at your highest level. I'll provide cutting-edge tools, tips, and tactics to increase your performance and productivity, as well as the best tools to reset and recover from your day. You'll learn about the different "Time

Types" of people and how to best communicate and perform with each type.

Together, we will clean out the time toxins, calendar contaminants, and "time management" junk that are blocking you from performing at your best. This shift in mindset will forever change your relationship, performance, and perception of time. It will show you how to put your time to work for you.

You don't have to wait your entire life to have the long-term happiness and success you deserve. You can have it right now and every day forward from now on!

Time is your ultimate resource.

It's *your time*! You own it. You control it.

It's your time, right now, to *make your move.*

Let's get started. Adding time to your life and life to your time.

DOWNLOADS

To ensure this process is tailored to you, *The Time Cleanse* is filled with interactive charts, worksheets, and more. I have made all worksheets available for download since you may need additional room to write in your answers or you may prefer not to write in your book at all. Each time you see this download symbol, know that you can head to www.timecleanse.com/book and download that page for yourself.

PART I
PREPARE

CHAPTER

1

A Matter of Time

Time is indeed our greatest currency.
To use it as best we can, to have as much fun as we can,
and to love as strongly as we can
because we never know when our time will be up.
—Dwayne Johnson

THINK ABOUT YOUR LIFE TODAY. NOW IMAGINE IF YOU had all the time you want and need. What could you accomplish? What if the amount of time that made a difference in your life was just one hour a day?

How would you spend just one more hour each day . . .

- Being with your loved ones and friends?

- Reinvesting in high-dollar business activities?

- Getting fit and healthy?

- Quieting your mind and balancing your spirit?

- Reading your favorite book or watching a favorite movie?

- Starting a side business?

- Eating at a new favorite restaurant?

- Getting extra sleep?

- Listening to music?

- Giving back?

Think about how your life would change if you had that extra hour every day to spend however you wanted.

That's 365 hours per year doing something that totally enriches your life and brings you joy and happiness.

That's 1,000 hours every three years doing something you *love*!

One hour can be the difference between a life worth living with purpose, hope, and happiness versus a life where you are strapped to the hamster wheel of stress, anxiety, and dissatisfaction.

The quality of your life is determined by how you choose to use your time.

Now before you start to beat yourself up, there is a reason why there is a gap between the hours you have and the ones you want and need to really enjoy life. Your time, energy, and focus have been hijacked by today's 24/7 connection to technology, constant distractions, and endless opportunities of instant gratification and stimulation. It's truly not your fault. It's your approach to time that's the reason—it's completely outdated.

Time is the only reason you are not living your full potential. Think about it. Why are you not going to the gym? Not making more sales calls? Not dating to find *the* one? Not enjoying a vacation? Not volunteering? The list goes on and on . . .

The number one searched "self-help" phrase on Google is not about money; it's not about fitness; it's not even about sex. The most searched self-help phrase on the internet is about *time*.

The Pew Research Center surveyed middle-class Americans about their number one priority. In response, 68 percent of people ranked having free time most important, which is quite revealing when the other areas of importance include having children (62 percent), having a successful career (59 percent), being married (55 percent), or being wealthy (12 percent).[1]

If time is so important to all of us, then why don't we invest more in mastering it? The simple answer is this: We're still relying on outdated time management tools that no longer work and have left us feeling hopeless and stuck and believing things can't be different.

What we need now is to upgrade our thinking when it comes to *performing* with time. With the speed that our lives are now moving at, we must evolve to keep pace with our modern, technology-driven world. That's what *The Time Cleanse* is all about.

If you are reading this book, it is not by accident. If you have been struggling, feel stuck, have hit a wall, or know you inherently have more potential than you're consistently utilizing, then you are ready for a breakthrough with *time*.

HAPPINESS AND SUCCESS

Happiness expert Shawn Achor, author of *The Happiness Advantage*, says, "Our most commonly held formula for success is broken. Conventional wisdom holds that if we work hard, we will be more successful, and if we are more successful, then we'll be happy."[2]

We've all been told that success comes from a great formal education, unbelievable talent, the right connections, and a winning personality. Luck and being in the right place at the right time also contribute to this message.

Societal standards, reality television, and the media have programmed us to believe that we have to have a million dollars in the bank, an amazing home, six-pack abs, the perfect relationship, a powerful career, and an expensive car in order to be happy. But this is a lie, an illusion. None of that is completely true, and it has us using and spending time in the wrong way.

Spending our precious time chasing false ideas of success drains our strength and energy, while also making us feel inadequate. It impedes our happiness and growth, our understanding of ourselves and others. And most importantly, it can lock us into a struggle where we constantly fight with time, claiming and believing it to be our greatest adversary and often the one thing that keeps us from achieving our personal happiness and success.

Don't get me wrong. I want you to have it all, and this book will help you get it; but I also want you to realize that the idea of success you may be working toward is not the true definition of success. It's not the source of *your* long-term happiness. I will help you uncover what's really important to you, which might even surprise you. In my opinion, success is consistently progressing toward a more enjoyable life connecting with your true talents and gifts. It's progressing toward whatever you think is important and understanding that this will change at different stages in your life. Only you can define what actually makes you successful and happy—and it should be nonnegotiable. It should reflect in every way what you are committed to having in your life, and it should serve as your GPS to help you get all that you desire and deserve.

If you truly want success, your measure should be in progress, not perfection. Progress is *the* essential ingredient in realizing success. When we're making progress, we're motivated to keep going; we're happy and feel good about life. And consistent progress is directly related to how you use and perform *with* your time.

The truth is that we all want gratification and success—and the faster the better. We are addicted to speed. We want our bank accounts to grow, our investments to accelerate, and our careers to advance quickly; we want to get into shape in days, have an instant loving relationship, and own our dream house at an early age. We want so much as *quickly* as we can imagine it. But what's just as important along with speed and achievement is enjoying the ride itself. The key here is that *your success is directly related to making the most out of your time.*

Time is our most valuable, precious, and limited commodity. But we make the mistake of throwing it away, not protecting it, pretending it's unlimited, and we treat it as if it were the same as any other commodity, but it is not. We can, however, change how we use it and with whom and where we spend it. But once we run out of time . . . there is no way to get more. It's game over!

There are plenty of things in life you can go without, but time is not one of them. You can live for weeks without food, days without water, and even minutes without air. But you cannot live for one second without time, and that's true no matter who you are. No amount of influence, power, or money can change the fact.

Time is life itself.

IN MY CORNER

I watched boxing as I grew up and was always fascinated by it. I loved seeing the big heavyweight fights and admiring the courage and power those guys had. They seemed like superheroes to me. I wanted to box when I was a kid, but I couldn't convince my mom to let me. I can still hear her voice, "You're not boxing as long as I have anything to do with it. When you turn 18, I can't control you, but until then . . ."

The moment I turned 18, I walked into my first boxing gym. It was in the basement of this old rec center outside of Chicago. The smell of sweat wafted through the air. You could hear the rapid rhythms of the speed bags being hit, the pounding of the heavy bags, and the ring buzzers going off. All this was background noise behind coaches yelling at their fighters. And it was all music to my ears. God was shining on me that day because that was the day I met Tom Delaney.

Tom Delaney was a Greyhound bus driver, Irish, in his early fifties, with blue eyes and a beer belly. When I met him, I was almost knocked out by his aroma of Old Spice cologne and sweat. Tom immediately took me under his wing, and it was one of the greatest gifts I've ever received. You see, he was able to see something in me that I hadn't yet seen in myself. I was an angry kid. I had doubts about who I was and if I was good enough. Tom saw all of that, as well as my talent. He had this unique ability to connect with me in a way that motivated and pushed me, while also nurturing that talent with compassion.

Right from the start, I wanted to get in the ring and spar. I was ready to let loose some of the anger and frustration I had been holding onto for years. I had been waiting so long to test myself. I was angry at the world and wanted to let it out. He just laughed and said, "Everything in time, my friend."

We started with the foundation—how to stand and throw the basic punch combinations, hit the heavy bag and the speed bag, and skip rope. Tom was conditioning my body to perform. Every workout was based on time—three minutes of work followed by one minute of rest. Boxing and this new three-to-one timing were different from all the sports I'd played up to this point, and this was the first sport I engaged in that wasn't a team sport.

Boxing requires you to give maximum exertion, then rest and repeat for multiple rounds. This was how Tom was preparing me for upcoming boxing competitions. I was in a hurry to always move on to the next thing, so I could begin sparring.

I was constantly watching the clock. Workouts seemed like an eternity, and I was struggling with the training. After a few weeks, Tom pulled me aside and said, "Watched pots don't boil." I had no idea what he meant, but he continued, "Big Steve, you learn really quickly, and you have great raw skills, but if you keep watching the clock, your mind will be distracted and the workouts will feel longer and harder. Here is what you need to do: Just focus on what you're working on. Your jab or combinations; just keep focusing on that. Whatever you're doing, time will take care of itself. It doesn't need you watching it. Just listen to the bell for when to work and when to rest, and your time will fly. You will have more fun, and your performance will improve quickly. But if you keep looking at the clock, . . . you might get clocked by a punch you never saw coming." I remember he laughed. He always had a good sense of wise-old-man humor.

This sage advice forced me to focus on what I was doing—and in the end, he was right. It was more fun, I got better faster, and time passed quickly.

While these were big pluses, what really got my attention was that my experience with time had shifted—I quit thinking about time and became fully present. I was fully in the moment and completely focused on the experience of *being* a boxer.

Over a short amount of time, with his coaching, I made it to two Golden Glove finals, the first one after only six months of training at 19 years of age in Chicago. The second final was one year later in Springfield, Illinois. One year after that, I won the Illinois State Heavyweight Championship.

The thing about Tom that really made all this success possible for me was the fact that he was always in my corner. No matter whether we were in or out of the ring, or if I won or lost. Tom was there. His skills as a boxing coach were tremendous, but that paled in comparison to what an amazing human being he was. Tom lived his life in a simple but powerful way. He was generous with his kindness, always looked at life with an optimistic view, had the patience and intuition to see the good qualities in people, and brought out their full potential. But most of all, he had a huge heart, and was always present and willing to help those who needed it with the time he had.

LESSONS LEARNED

Here are the lessons I learned from my time with Tom:

- Time takes care of itself if you take care of it.
- Being present alters time perception, performance, and fun.
- You can get clocked if you are distracted.
- There is a timing for success.
- Time and performance need to work in synchronicity.
- We all should have a Tom Delaney in our corner.

TIME-STEALING TECHNOLOGY

Technology is one of the primary things hijacking our time in the modern world. Fortunately, there are strategies I'll show you to safeguard your time and take it back.

The ability to choose *how* we use our time is the greatest gift we have under our control.

The Powerbroker: Choice

Having the ability to choose gives us the ultimate power to pursue our most important hopes, dreams, happiness, and unique purpose—to create meaningful lives for what matters most to us.

With our constant connectivity, distractions, and drive to stay busy and get more things done, our ability to choose where we use our time has largely been lost. We don't have the time or take the time to stop, pause, and reflect on what we truly want.

This frantic pace has us no longer consciously thinking for ourselves. We're operating on autopilot and letting our devices and environment do the thinking for us—from our GPS telling us what turns to make, to the endless suggestions our devices make to us about what to listen to, watch, do, buy, wear, eat, and act on in our lives.

The most dangerous part of this is that it's been happening slowly, methodically, and mostly outside of our conscious awareness. You don't even know that your choice is being stolen along with your time.

To have the life we want, we need to get back in the driver's seat with our time. First, we have to remember we have choices. Second, we have to make the right choices that are in alignment with what we truly want in life and what really matters the most to us.

In his groundbreaking research on human behavior, Dr. Martin Seligman coined the condition just described as "learned helplessness."[3] His research showed that after repeated negative stimuli, helplessness can be learned by believing that you have little or no control. As a result, people become conditioned to forget that they have the ability to choose at all.

This vicious condition is today's modern version of learned helplessness. Even our screen sizes are affecting our choices and can influence feelings of helplessness. Recent research out of Harvard Business School by Amy Cuddy and Maarten Bos looked at how screen size affects behavior.[4]

The researchers had participants do work on devices of different sizes. What they found was a correlation between more expansive body postures and the use of a larger device (MacBook Pro laptop or iMac desktop) that led to more power-related behaviors, such as assertiveness. However, people who used smaller devices (iPod Touch or iPad) showed significantly less assertiveness. The result: the larger the screen, the more assertive. When it comes to our devices, size does matter.

This discovery about screen size is quite startling when you look at how much time we spend on our phones and how this can affect our choices. If you're primarily interacting with a small screen all day long, be aware that it can be influencing you to be less assertive in your choices.

How Tech Steals Your Time

> All of our minds can be hijacked.
> Our choices are not as free as we think they are.
> —TRISTAN HARRIS

Before we dive into how tech steals your time, let me first say that tech devices have significantly improved the quality of our lives as well as our ability to perform both in business and in life. They can be a game changer when we know how to use them for the positive benefits they offer.

But, when you look closely at your life, you'll see that one of the biggest hijackers of your time is your phone. Our devices are increasingly designed to support interaction with apps that influence our thinking and actions, which takes us deeper into the rabbit hole. The tech industry is influencing your behavior in ways that most people are not even aware of. It is what is now being called "brain hacking."

Technology is now directing what 2 billion-plus people are seeing, thinking, and believing most of the day. Much of that information is targeted to influence your specific preferences, with the goal of influencing your time. Don't believe me? Research shows that the average person checks his or her phone up to 150 times a day![5]

Tristan Harris, former Google designer and founder of the Center for Humane Technology, has spent a decade understanding the invisible influences that hijack human thinking and action. Harris explains, "Just like the food industry manipulates our innate biases for salt, sugar, and fat with perfectly engineered combinations, Instagram, Twitter, [and] Facebook are built under the 'variable rewards' scheme. The tech industry coerces our innate biases for: 'Social Reciprocity' (we're built to get back to others), 'Social Approval' (we're built to care what others think of us), 'Social Comparison' (how we're doing with respect to our peers), and 'Novelty-Seeking' (we're built to seek surprises over the predictable)."[6]

Additionally, our addiction to being constantly connected has created an entirely new and unique fear: the fear of missing out, or FOMO. While we may think we are missing out on something important, we are actually missing out on being present in our own lives. We are constantly worrying about other people, places, and things instead of being in the moment. This is all time you can't get back.

Harris presents the idea that our phones are like slot machines. Slot machines are highly addictive and rely on intermittent variable rewards. Each pull of the lever gives you the opportunity to win or lose, which highly stimulates the brain as it anticipates the outcome. Research shows that slot machines make more money in the United States than baseball, movies, and theme parks combined.

Each and every time we look at our phones or computers for a text, e-mail, or Facebook notification, we are pulling the lever of a slot machine that floods the mind and body with dopamine and other feel-good neurotransmitters that hardwire our addictions to these devices.

In a 2016 study, researchers used an app to capture every engagement we have with our phones in one day. The results showed that we tap, type, swipe, or click our phones an average of 2,617 times a day! That's over four hours a day spent on our phones!

We need to realize that every click, swipe, or tap equals time, and we are giving away much more of it than we realize.

Knowledge is power when it comes to our time, and technology and advertisers have been focused on influencing our buying decisions for decades. This is nothing new—but we also weren't walking into a store at all hours of the day and night. Today, with unlimited connectivity, we are constantly open to the influence of advertisers 24 hours a day. So how do we make better choices and stop allowing time-wasters like our phones to take over so much of our time?

I believe the answer is mindfulness—which is *being fully aware and present in the moment.*

MINDFULNESS

Live the actual moment. Only this actual moment is life.
—Thích Nhất Hạnh

In today's world, "mindfulness" has become a new buzzword that you hear from your local yoga studio to the latest political speech. But I'm here to simplify and demystify this often-misunderstood concept and show you exactly how it applies to you and the Time Cleanse process.

When I talk about mindfulness in the pages of this book, I am referring to *being in the moment where you are fully aware of your thoughts, your physical presence, your emotions, your senses, and all that is around you—without judgment and with a sense of curiosity.* But there's more . . .

In *The Time Cleanse*, we expand and build on the traditional viewpoint and definition of mindfulness from the perspective of how to perform with time, which I call "Timefulness"—*being fully present in the moment improving the quality, experience, and performance with your time.*

As you work through the book and the Time Cleanse process, you will hear me refer to the concept of Timefulness. This doesn't replace mindfulness. Instead, think of Timefulness as a specialized version of it focusing on being present with time and creating the results you want with it—*being mindful with time.*

With this definition in mind, let's explore the question of why being in the moment is not just important, it's everything! It enriches every experience and allows you to connect more deeply with life and others—getting you back in the driver's seat of making conscious choices that help you activate and realize your full potential. It allows you to be present to what matters most, when it matters most, which is always right now.

By being present, you can expand and direct your use of time. It is the ultimate secret weapon in doing, being, and having more. It's your key to creating meaningful relationships, overall happiness, ultimate purpose, and greater achievement in the areas of life that matter the most to you. And I'm going to teach you exactly how to do it in the Time Cleanse.

In today's hyperconnected world, most people are in a constant battle throughout their day, which is usually worrying about the future or reflecting on the past and how it could have been different. All this back-and-forth between the past and future can eat up your time and distract you. Not being present is one of the biggest stealers of your time.

By being mindful—or Timeful—you give yourself the gift of being able to come back to the present moment after you've been distracted. Being present allows you to alter your quality, experience, and performance with time.

When it comes to business, Timefulness helps multitaskers be more focused, salespeople close more deals, managers be more efficient and effective, and leaders be more motivating, creative, and inspiring. It gives you the opportunity to stop and take a step back to gain a bigger perspective on your sense of self and surroundings. It also provides you with a clearer picture of how you are using your time.

When you train yourself to be fully present in the moment, you take charge of time in a new way and are able to call on your talents, intuition, creativity, and highest self. The more present you are, the higher you perform. I have seen this over and over with executives, CEOs, entrepreneurs, military leaders, pro athletes, and celebrities that I have trained in mindfulness, meditation, and Timefulness.

Mindfulness Through Meditation

Many people have the misconception that mindfulness and the practice of meditation are ways to enter into some sort of "magical state" that they can't be good at. That is simply not the case. Instead, meditation is a simple process that everyone can do. While there are different types of meditation, the basic purpose of each is to teach you to focus and refocus your attention and awareness to the present moment.

MEDITATION

Here is a simple way to meditate:

Begin by sitting quietly in a relaxed, upright position with your eyes closed. Pay attention to your breathing by putting your awareness on your belly, noticing it rising and falling from your diaphragm, near your belly button. Now notice your breath as you inhale and exhale naturally, with your belly rising and falling with each breath. As you begin, it's normal to have wandering thoughts or feelings come up—just return to focusing on your breath at your belly. Be with those thoughts or feelings without any judgment. You are not trying to create any particular result or state, but instead you are being with the thoughts and feelings that surface and acknowledging them for what they are, nothing more.

The real key to meditating is training yourself to come back to your breath after you have become distracted. This exercise produces the "state" of being present (mindful), and with practice, it will become a "trait," a regular way of living and being. It puts you in control of your time by now having the ability to respond consciously to the choices you make versus reacting habitually without thinking.

 To help you get started, I have provided a guided meditation that's available for download at www.timecleanse.com/book.

The research on the positive effects of mindfulness is substantial and proves that mindfulness has the ability to do all of the following:

- Diminish and manage stress

- Decrease anxiety, pain, and depression

- Increase cognitive functioning

- Increase happiness

- Increase performance

- Create positive brain chemistry

- Experience greater emotional regulation

- Slow the aging process[7]

When you begin to implement mindfulness in all aspects of your life, you are no longer controlled by automatic negative thoughts or emotions that don't serve you. It allows you to see beyond your past, create more choices, expand the possibilities in your life, and take control of your time. Mindfulness opens the space to seeing abundance, opportunity, and the way to get there.

These benefits also extend outward from ourselves as well to greater compassion and empathy for others. Living life from this state allows for greater connection and relatedness, enriching the experience we have with everyone we engage with.

When you're totally present, you have the "direct experience" of life. For instance, it's the middle of the summer and you're sitting on a dock by the ocean: You're feeling the warm sun on your face; you're enjoying the breeze and view of the ocean, smelling the fresh ocean air, and listening to the seagulls—you're being present.

Compare this with sitting on the same dock, but all you're thinking about is "Did I turn the stove off?" "Why are my kids being so difficult?" "I can't remember if I sent that e-mail." "Am I going to get that promotion?" For most of us, this "narrative state" is how we live day to day—it's our default setting.

When we are in this narrative state, we are constantly thinking about what we are doing. Our ability to fully access our senses is limited; our cognitive ability shrinks, as well as our ability to handle stress. This narrative is what hijacks our time, increases our anxiety, and reduces our productivity and happiness. The good news is that mindfulness can reduce and eliminate many of these issues.

Present, Pause, and Proceed

To counteract what is likely your natural narrative, reactive, and distractive state, I developed a three-step Timefulness performance technique called Present, Pause, and Proceed. It was inspired by the teachings of one of my early mentors, Dr. Pat Allen, a pioneer in the study of human relationships and communication.

Try the following steps to regulate stressful situations, handle negative thoughts and feelings, make better decisions, and perform at an optimal level:

Step 1. Present

Notice negative thought patterns and sensations occurring in your body; then take a deep, diaphragmatic breath and exhale.

> EXAMPLE
>
> You might notice a tightness in your chest, pressure in your head, or pain in your back or stomach.

Step 2. Pause

Begin to differentiate the emotions and mental thoughts from the sensations in your body. Identify and label them.

> EXAMPLE
>
> As you become aware of the pain in your stomach, you realize that what's behind that sensation of pain is the emotion of being "anxious." Or the negative thoughts in your mind have a feeling of anger behind them. Now that you've identified an emotion, ask yourself, "What do I have that I don't want?" or "What don't I have that I want?"

Step 3. Proceed

Take another diaphragmatic breath. Determine and focus on thoughts and actions that are in alignment with what you want or don't want. Next, take action steps to shift into a more resourceful mental-emotional state.

> EXAMPLE
> Go for a walk, meditate, talk to a friend, do some internal reflection, and/or journal your next positive action steps. This will allow you the time to reset and reengage to a higher-performing state.

By using the three-step Present, Pause, and Proceed Timefulness technique, you will break the pattern of the old automatic reactivity and immediately be able to reset your mental and emotional state to take charge and perform at your highest level.

Being present allows you to optimize your time for what matters most in your life. To do that, you first need to understand just what your current relationship with time is and how to perform with it for maximum results—and that's exactly what we'll do in Chapter 2.

CHAPTER

2

Understanding Your Relationship with Time

> You're not here to survive this,
> you're here to take charge of it.
> —U.S. Navy SEALs

TIME IS THE ESSENCE OF LIFE. IT IS EVERYTHING YOU will do, get, or become. And in my opinion, along with using it to create happiness and success, it has one unique purpose: to create memories that add life to your time and time to your life. Ultimately, it's leaving a lasting legacy that you're proud of.

Somewhere along the way we moved away from this philosophy. Our lives began to move so fast, we went into autopilot and began serving time trying to just survive the day. If you are like most people today, there's more and more to do with less and less time. It seems like there's never enough time to get everything done because you're constantly being pulled in so many directions, interrupted and distracted all at the same time. We are stuck in a crazy, multitasking, chaotic world and under tremendous pressure to perform and produce 24/7. We've become addicted to this pace. We're afraid to slow down for a second, much less to take a vacation, because we fear we won't hit our goals, that someone else will take our place, and worse yet, that we will fail in our lives.

We crave more and more, yet we end up feeling less and less satisfied. We feel more unbalanced, stressed, and fatigued while being completely disconnected from our true purpose.

Many of us have become addicted to the constant activity, technology, and connectivity of our lives. We often operate according to old ideas, habits, and behaviors without reassessing where our time and efforts are best placed. We don't take the time to stop and ask ourselves, "Am I going in the right direction in the right way?" or "Is this the best use of my time and talent?" All of this directly affects our relationship to time, performance, and our overall life success.

The good news is that there is a completely different way to live in relationship and performance with *time*. One that supports and helps you do, be, and have what you want—which I will show you through the Time Cleanse process.

But first, I have a few questions for you. What is your relationship with time? Is it on your side and working for you? Do you have plenty of time? Do you feel you're not rushed, can get everything done, and have lots of energy?

Or is it the opposite? Does time feel like something that's working against you or something you're fighting? Do you feel like you're constantly rushing, under pressure, and stressed and wishing there was more time in your day?

After working with thousands of people, I've learned one crucial thing: that most people today have a relationship with time that is very unsupportive and adversarial. This is caused by outdated ideas and myths we have been led to believe about time, performance, and success.

Just as technology has changed how we live our lives, so must we adapt and shift how to use time today. What most people don't realize is that they are missing out on their full potential because they don't understand how to effectively use time in today's technology-driven world. Time, used in the right way, is your ultimate partner in creating the life you want.

TIME PRESSURE

Psychologist Hendrie Weisinger offers insight about time pressure in his book *Performing Under Pressure*. Weisinger contends that most people confuse stress and pressure. Stress occurs when there are more demands than can be met by resources—time, effort, and money. And pressure is related to the perceived value of what is at stake, most specifically as an outcome dependent on your performance related to time.

In Weisinger's view, when we don't understand the critical difference, "it deletes valuable psychological and physical resources. We lose the ability to think clearly and our energy becomes misplaced as we continue to act as though everyday activities are a matter of life and death."[1]

When it comes to performing with time, it's important to know the difference so that you are not inadvertently adding more pressure to your daily life than is needed. No one performs better under increased time pressure, and the Time Cleanse will help you shift that.

The Effects of Time Pressure

Try something with me. Go ahead and *take a deep breath*—be sure to breathe all the way in. *Now hold it.* Imagine working, competing, socializing (*keep holding your breath*), parenting, managing, exercising (*keep holding it*), problem solving, meditating, journaling (*keep holding it*), and try to relax while thinking about all of this (*keep holding it*). How does it feel? (*Hold it just a little longer.*) Now imagine you have to go through your day like this, going to work, being with your family, commuting, and more.

Breathe out.

Every day when you operate with time in this way, you create that same pressure you likely felt as you held your breath. This is what happens consciously, and many times subconsciously, out of your awareness every day and leads to ongoing fatigue, stress, anxiety, and overwhelm. Is it any wonder you are exhausted by the end of the day?

An interesting study out of Case Western University was conducted to measure the effect of perceived time pressure on completing a task. Two groups were given the same amount of time to complete tasks. One group was told it had sufficient time to complete the task, while the other was told it did not have sufficient time for the same task. In actuality, both groups had enough time for completion. The group that was told it didn't have enough time consistently performed lower. The researchers concluded that perceived time pressure caused lower performance.[2]

Not only is perceived time pressure affecting our performance, but there is even evidence that it is affecting our health. A study from the Women's Health Australia project focused on a sample of 1,580 women who perceived time pressure in regard to its effect on their ability to eat healthier foods. Forty-one percent of the women in the study reported that time pressure did affect their food choices, which resulted in a lower intake of fruits and vegetables and an increase in fast-food consumption.[3]

The health issues of time pressure, seen as early as 1959, continue to be implicated in cardiovascular concerns. Cardiologists Meyer Friedman and Ray Rosenman deemed that one of the top three characteristics of type A personalities is "a heightened sense of time urgency that is linked to increased incidence of cardiovascular disease."[4] Time pressure is one of the biggest rising issues today, severely affecting our performance and health, in both life and business.

But I am here to show you that there is a different way, a better way where time can work for you, where you can live and work without the constraints of time pressure and you can perform at your full potential with the Time Cleanse process.

Time is your most critical resource and your most important relationship.

The Time Cleanse starts with an understanding and acknowledgment of that truth. From my research, over 95 percent of people have an unsupportive and adversarial relationship with time, feeling like time is "against" them. They feel like a victim of time.

Understanding Your Current Relationship with Time

Read the following statements and put a check mark by the statements you most relate to:

- ❏ Rushed or out of control at times during the day

- ❏ Distracted from the task at hand

- ❏ Fatigued during or at the end of the day

- ❏ Worried about getting everything done

- ❏ Stressed about the day

- ❏ Under time pressure while working

- ❏ Like you must multitask to get everything done

- ❏ That your to-do list never gets completed

Or do you feel . . .

- ❏ In control of your day

- ❏ Energized throughout the day with normal fluctuations

- ❏ Focused on the tasks at hand

- ❏ Confident in the day and completing what you need to do

- ❏ That you have plenty of time rather than just enough time to get everything done

- ❏ Calm and fulfilled at the end of the day

- ❏ Mindful and present in the moment during activities

- ❏ Accomplished because you completed your to-do list by the end of the day

If you identified more with the first group of statements than the second, your relationship with time is adversarial and nonsupportive right now. If you identified more with the second group, your relationship with time is more aligned and supportive to you. This exercise is an important one to create awareness around your current relationship with time today, so you can make improvements where you desire.

LIVING IN ABUNDANCE VERSUS SCARCITY

> The great dividing line between success and failure
> can be expressed in five words: "I did not have time."
> —ROBERT J. HASTINGS

How often do you find yourself saying:

- "If my schedule allows."

- "There simply aren't enough hours in the day."

- "If only I'd gotten another hour of sleep."

- "I never have enough time."

- "If I could just get caught up."

- "Where did the time go?"

- "I'm so behind, I'll never get it done."

- "I'd love to talk, but I've got to run."

- "When I have the time."

- "If time allows."

Now ask yourself this simple question: "Who is time?" When I asked myself this question years ago, I realized I am time and always have been.

In order to change the way we understand and operate based on this different and beneficial way of thinking about time, we have to accept the fact that our performance with time comes from the choices we make. What we choose to say yes and no to and what we decide to do determine and indicate when and where we use our time. When we believe time is outside of us and controlling us, we live in a constant state of scarcity and victimhood without even realizing it.

After working with thousands of people, I have seen every version of a time excuse offered as the number one reason people aren't finding the success, happiness, and achievement they desire. This widespread faulty thinking is the exact reason people are struggling, stalled, or stuck.

Gay Hendricks tells the perfect story, which I paraphrase here, to illustrate this thinking in his book *The Big Leap*.[5] He puts you in the mindset by asking you to imagine that you are working from home and your eight-year-old child comes in and asks, "Will you play catch with me?" and you reply, "I don't have time to do that right now. I'm working." Now imagine the exact same scenario, only this time your child says, "Look, I just cut my foot. Can you help me?" You likely are going to jump up, leave your work behind, and immediately take care of your child.

When you compare those two situations, you realize it's not *time* that's to blame; it's *your choices or priorities with time*. We can *always* make or find time when something is our priority.

So really, time always comes down to choice—not time. It's very important that you understand this distinction as we move forward in the Time Cleanse and that you let go of the illusion that time is something outside of you controlling you. It's absolutely not. Time comes from you, and you're 100 percent responsible for your time—and it's my commitment and honor to show you how to use it.

Let's take a look at where you're making time excuses.

Make a list of ways in which you are currently making time excuses. This is an opportunity to be completely honest with yourself and shift your thinking for not doing, being, or having what you want in life because of time.

1. _____

2. _____

3. _____

4. _____

5. _____

It's time to stop using time as the reason why you can't do something or haven't done something. Change your language to reflect the fact that you are choosing to use time in a particular way: "I'm choosing to do this," or "I'm choosing to do that." *You are time*, and as soon as you accept that, you will be 100 percent in control of what you do and your destiny.

My personal mantra is this:

> I'm 100 percent responsible for my time.
> I own it, I control it, and it comes from me!

TIME PERFORMANCE VERSUS TIME MANAGEMENT

> Just a few words on time management:
> forget all about it.
> —TIM FERRISS

We all have heard a lot about time management. Most time management philosophies were developed before the advancement of technology, when phones were connected to the wall by a cord.

Time management is stuck in the past and operates from a narrow mindset that there is a fixed amount of time within which we all must operate. Our fixed amount of time is 60 seconds, 60 minutes, 24 hours, and 168 hours a week. That's it. That is the time we have—and we need to make the most of it and do the best we can with it. Just as technology is rapidly advancing, you, too, must upgrade to a new way of using time.

That kind of thinking does not create a peaceful mental state or help us perform at our highest level. Plus, most of us can't stay organized enough to "manage" our time every hour of every day. That's just not how real life works.

Time management programs offer tools, skills, and tactics that focus on what you can get done *based on* time. In traditional time management, time is considered a scarce resource always ticking away, and its true focus is task completion within a fixed unit of time. With this mindset, time is an outside force that we have no influence over except to get good at managing it.

As I said in this book's Introduction, your goal isn't to manage any of your relationships. You have to connect, work, and flow with them, not manage them. It's the same with time. You don't want to manage time; you want to perform with it in a positive way that supports your goals and what you want in life.

Now let's imagine time in a different way: one where you are in control, direct, and perform with time; one where you have a positive relationship with time. Time becomes your ally, a trusted friend that wants what you want, can provide what's best for you, and will consistently move you toward what matters most to you at all times.

This is the mindset behind *time performance* and the Time Cleanse system. With this way of operating, time becomes a supportive relationship that enables you to bring focus, energy, and attention to what's most important in your business and life. By doing this, you are mastering time, not living as a victim of time.

The distinction between the two mindsets, as well as the systems that support each, is that they operate from an entirely different *relationship* with time that creates the environment in which you live.

It's time to learn a smarter, more efficient, and more productive way to take back what's rightfully yours, to *reclaim* time, perform with it, and transform your life.

In order to fully understand why these operating systems are so vastly different, let's take a look at the two mindsets:

TIME MANAGEMENT	TIME PERFORMANCE
Objective is to get things done	Objective is accelerating performance while getting things done
Time is fixed and scarce	Time is expandable and abundant
Mindset that time acts on you	Mindset that time comes from you
Time is something to manage	Time is something to perform with
Focuses on time itself	Focuses on your relationship with it
All hours are equal	You can alter the quality, experience, and performance of an hour
Task and priority focused	Life purpose, enjoyment, and satisfaction focused

By understanding the difference between these two mindsets and shifting from one to the other, you will increase the quality, experience, and performance with your time. In this new mindset, you will think, engage, and perform in a way that creates new possibilities with every hour you have.

As a performance coach, I work with people who are motivated to close their performance gaps. What is a performance gap? It's actually very simple. It's where you are right now versus where you want to be, and closing this gap with speed is the core benefit of the Time Cleanse process. I hope you are motivated to close this gap and find new ways to do things. I bet that's why you picked this book up.

In my experience, successful people are the ones who are the most motivated to gain more success. They are open to imagining how life can continue to improve and advance, and they love to find new ways to bring forth their best skills and talents. Even highly accomplished people who are top performers often overlook their relationship with time as a vital factor—I'm here to change that.

Once you shift your mindset to time performance rather than time management, you'll experience the myriad benefits that emerge including . . .

- Increased relaxation

- Less pressure

- More creativity

- Improved cognitive function

- Increased energy

- Access to a flow state

- Freedom to do more

- More productive in less time

- Overall higher performance

These are all amazing ways to feel versus the pressure of trying to manage your time.

Shifting Your Mindset from Managing to Performing

Here's a look at a typical day with *time management* as your focus:

1. Before you start your workday, the pressure of how you are going to get everything done is beginning to rise.

2. You know from experience that it takes 20 minutes to get from home to work.

3. You "manage" your time and give yourself exactly 20 minutes to get to the office. You also cram as much as you can in the time leading up to the exact time you "plan" to leave.

4. Whoops, everything ran over (it almost always does), and now you are hustling to get in the car—your time pressure continues to build.

5. Once in the car, you are tense; there's traffic, and you're sure to be late.

6. You rush to get to the parking lot, but you're only focused on the fact that you can't get there in time. You start to say to yourself, "I'll arrange my calendar differently tomorrow, so I won't be late."

7. You sit down at your desk before your first meeting, but you're off your game. Your body and mind are caught in a stressful state—all because of your perceived time pressure.

And here is a look at your day with *time performance* as your focus:

1. Before you start your workday, knowing you're in charge of your time, you are calm, focused, and excited to engage in your work.

2. You start your day knowing that whatever comes your way, you can adjust accordingly. You focus your awareness and mindset on what you want to engage in, what you want to accomplish, and what commitments you have at specific times.

3. You imagine the flow of the day, giving particular attention to times when you need to move to a new location and how you will travel from one place to another without pressure.

4. You ensure you have all the resources to get to work and the meetings you've scheduled. You have a full gas tank, and you've planned your route. You take things you might enjoy along the way, such as water, snacks, and/or your favorite music.

5. As you make your way to work, you hit traffic. You remain calm knowing you'll get there when you get there and that adding time pressure to yourself will only stress you out.

6. You end up arriving at work with extra time, stress free, focused, and ready to engage.

How to Alter Time

Now that you understand the difference between time management and time performance, I turn to Einstein and what he taught us through his theory of relativity. In order to alter time, Einstein proposed that you need to occupy space in a different way. To put this into perspective, let's look at a quote from Einstein: "Put your hand on a hot stove for a minute and it seems like an hour. Sit with your beloved for an hour and it seems like a minute."

When your hand is on a hot stove, you become focused on not occupying the space you're in. Then, every part of you is focused on retracting from the space you're occupying because of the pain you're feeling from the stove. This retracting of the space you're occupying causes time to slow or even stop. The more you retract, the more time slows.

This may sound familiar if you've ever had a job you didn't like. You just wanted the day to go quickly, but it seemed to go on and on. Your body was there, but mentally, you had removed yourself—retracting from being present—because of the discomfort and pain of the job. Time just dragged by.

Now on the flip side, when you're with your beloved, time flies because you are engaging and occupying space differently. You're focused on leaning toward and expanding into the space with your beloved. You're fully present mentally and physically in the space you're occupying. You and time are unified, and hours seem like minutes.

Think about when you're in a deep conversation, or singing, or playing your favorite sport, or experiencing something incredible. Time flies. This happens when you're engaged and fully present. In these moments, you are at one with time.

By being completely present, you change your quality with time, your experience of it, and how you perform with it. You're living with Timefulness.

TIME CLEANSE IN ACTION: SOPHIA'S STORY

Sophia was a senior executive at a major national bank. When I met her, she was constantly under time pressure, pushing herself to perform at superhuman levels to get more and more done every single day of every week. For example, she'd regularly drop off her dry cleaning, take her dog to the vet, return a dozen phone calls, and close a sale in a client meeting all before noon.

Don't get me wrong. Sophia was incredibly productive on a daily basis, but she never slowed down enough to think about what was really important. She was constantly fighting against the clock, living with a scarcity mindset, believing there just was never enough time. Her stress levels were now off the chart as she tried to perform everything the day required all by herself. Her coffee drinking turned to potent energy drinks as she began to rely more and more on caffeine just to keep up with her own unrelenting pace.

The constant time pressure began to affect her physically and emotionally as she began to gain weight and not sleep well. Until the Time Cleanse, she never stopped to ask herself if there were better ways to accomplish the things she was doing. Sophia kept powering through her days, but it came at a cost.

Sophia, like many of us, had been conditioned for many years to believe that time was something outside of her control, and she was constantly trying to manage it. As she progressed through the Time Cleanse process, she realized she had an adversarial relationship with time, fighting with it daily to get everything done. When it became clear that her constant and never-ending battle was a choice, she began laughing hysterically. This belief that time was her adversary had been driving her unnecessarily to a frenzied state that wasn't supporting her life. And when she learned that she was actually the source of her time and was in control of it, her time pressure instantly released and things began to shift. She could perform with it instead of trying to manage it.

Through the Time Cleanse, Sophia came to the realization that her health was most important to her. She then refocused and rebalanced her life and let go of the "busy work" she had previously demanded of herself. She started by delegating activities that didn't need her input or expertise—tasks like dropping off the dry cleaning, going to the vet, and doing online research—to her assistant.

These steps allowed her to reclaim 15 hours a week, which completely changed her life. She began a regular exercise program and was eating in a healthier way and stopped the extra energy drinks.

She was amazed at how quickly her stress faded once she took on a performance mindset—Timefulness. She now focused her energy and time on the things that mattered the most to her without her previous distractions. Time no longer was her evil adversary. Now she controlled time.

Most importantly, she now moved through each day without time pressure, allowing her to use her incredible focus on growing her business while improving her health and well-being. Now she is enjoying a more balanced, stress-free, productive life.

Once you've made the shift to time performance—knowing that time comes from you, that you create it, you control it, it's abundant, and you can have a positive relationship with it—it allows you to live free of stress and time pressure. You can change your quality, experience, and results with time by living in this new way in any area of your life.

CHAPTER

3

What Drives Your Life?

The two most important days of your life are the day you
were born and the day you find out why.
—Mark Twain

YOUR WHY

The bigger the "why" the easier the "how."
—Jim Rohn

CLIENTS COME TO ME WHEN THEY'RE STUCK,
stopped, or struggling to have the life they want or want to accelerate and
have more consistent results than they're getting—both in their business
and in their personal lives. One of the very first things I ask is, "What
are you committed to having?" That can be anything from their life purpose, specific business goal, to a life goal—which most people have a clear
understanding of, such as "building my business," "having a better relationship with my spouse," or "being healthy and fit."

Then I ask them the simple question, "Why do you want that?" The
typical response is a generalized answer with no deep emotional connection to their core motivation and purpose—and that has been pre-
programmed for so long that it doesn't have a current motivational
connection. This gap between their obvious answer and their core motiva-

tion is the primary reason why so many people get stuck, stop, struggle, or lack consistency and motivation.

Simon Sinek, one of the leading thinkers on this topic, tells us in his book *Start with Why*, "Everyone knows what they do 100 percent of the time. Some know how they do it. Very few people in organizations, in the world, and in their own personal life know *why* they do what they do."[1] His definition of "why" is "the purpose or cause; the single driving motivation for action." Knowing your own why is the key to connecting with the deep motivational centers of your brain that inspire action. Your why gets you to connect with your purpose. Your why then becomes your purpose identified.

Why Is Your "Why" So Important?

The answer to this question is:

1. **YOUR WHY GIVES MEANING TO EVERYTHING YOU DO.** You can appear to be successful on the outside, but if you are not internally aligned with your why, you will never truly feel satisfied in life.

2. **YOUR WHY DIRECTS AND GUIDES YOU.** Not only can your why give you meaning, it can also give you clear direction about where to go in life. It can help you make both big and small decisions and take the next step.

3. **YOUR WHY MOTIVATES YOU.** In life, there will be difficult times to go through. You may experience setbacks, rejection, and failure. In such situations, your why can give you the motivation you need to keep going. It also becomes your GPS in everything you do with your time.

4. **YOUR WHY MAKES YOUR TIME RELEVANT.** Connecting with your why ensures that you are using your gifts and talents in a way that connects with your true purpose, making a positive difference for you and the collective. It directs and maximizes your time

in a purposeful and meaningful way that gives relevance to everything you do.

CONNECTING WITH YOUR WHY

Here is the process: After asking "What am I committed to having?" simply ask yourself, "Why is that important to me?" It is essential to keep asking yourself the why question until you get to the core motivation of your purpose. This can happen quickly, but you must keep asking until you intuitively feel you have reached your core motivation. In this process, it is common to recycle previous answers, which is completely normal. By doing this, you're breaking through any of your subconscious barriers to get to your ultimate *why*.

Identify Your Why

I have a specific process you can use to uncover your purpose. It involves answering the questions below. I provided my own answers as a way for you to understand what the process is like:

- "What am I committed to having?"
  My answer: "To be the best researcher, speaker, and coach."

- "Why is this important to me?"
  My answer: "So I can feel good about helping people improve their lives."

- "Why is that important?"
  My answer: "So they feel someone is in their corner supporting them."

- "Why is that important?"
  My answer: "So they believe that they can have the life they want."

- "Why is that important?"
  My answer: "To help people discover and live their true purpose."

This last answer got me to the core of my true motivation.

Determining your why applies to specific goals in any area of your life. For every goal you have or everything you want to achieve, you need to know the why to align your efforts and motivations to achieve your goals. Here is an example.

I had a client come in for wellness and health issues that were affecting her business performance. Audrey is an executive in her late forties. She believed she had 20 pounds to lose and knew she was not in good physical condition.

When she walked in, she said, "I'm having some barriers to losing weight."

"What's your goal?" I asked.

"To lose 20 pounds."

"Why is that important to you?"

"Well, so I can feel good," she answered.

"Why is that important to you?"

"You know, so I can feel healthy."

"Why is that important to you?"

"I need to be more active to keep up with my kids."

"Why is that important to you?"

"Because my mother passed away when I was 20, and I want to be there well into adulthood for my kids."

I could literally see the shift reflected in her eyes. Audrey's purpose was not just about losing 20 pounds so she could be more active and feel better. Instead, her why for this particular goal was to be present and have an enriched and long life with her kids. When she realized that, she became highly motivated and easily lost all the weight after trying and failing in the past.

If I had let Audrey's purpose be to just lose some weight over time, she would have failed. There would have been no connection with the deep motivational centers of her brain, the area that motivates her to take action.

Therefore, as you progress in the Time Cleanse process, you'll see why it's important to connect your why with your values and goals to accelerate your performance and invest your time in what matters most to you.

It took nearly 15 years for me to realize the impact that Tom Delaney, my boxing coach, had on me. I had been living in Los Angeles for almost 15 years after moving there from Chicago. I was a professional coach helping individuals and businesses take their performance to the next level. Performance coaching was an emerging field when I began, and it was exciting to be at the forefront. My business was expanding, and I had the honor and opportunity to work with many top executives, CEOs, entrepreneurs, military leaders, pro athletes, and celebrities.

One day, just like any other, a client asked me a completely unexpected question that led me to a deep realization. A realization can be exciting, liberating, emotional, and painful. This one was all of that for me and more. My client asked who inspired me to be a coach and influenced me in my style. I thought for a moment, and I was embarrassed at the time not to have a good answer. I had trained with some of the top experts in the world, read hundreds of books, logged over 10,000 hours of coaching clients, learned from over a hundred coaches of different types and in different areas of expertise, but still did not have a solid answer. The question stayed with me. I began to look back over the years and immediately identified coaches I felt had the right intentions but as a coach just weren't very effective. Actually, a few of them were terrible. But we do learn something from bad experiences, and so in some ways they contributed to my sense of what not to do.

I kept thinking about who had really made a difference in my way of thinking and who had helped me find my unique path as a coach. Then the memory of the scent of Old Spice cologne mixed with sweat permeated my mind ... and Tom Delaney appeared. I laughed out loud. I had not seen him in years, but thinking of Tom opened a floodgate of memories as if it were yesterday.

Tom really understood me and knew how to connect with me in a way that motivated and inspired me to push myself and be my best.

He was ...

- **A GREAT LISTENER.** He was calm and present, and he could see things that others couldn't see.

- **FIRM.** He wasn't overly demanding, but he was still firm in his coaching and conviction, was flexible when needed, and always looked at how to make things happen, never focusing on why they couldn't.

- **PASSIONATE.** In fact, he was passionate beyond belief. He had a giant heart and was filled with compassion, always coming from the place of giving first (he always had a gym bag full of wraps and accessories he would give for free if someone was in need), and he was humble.

- **SYSTEMATIC.** He knew how to use time in the most effective and efficient way to maximize performance. He always sought out others if he thought they could coach some aspect better than he could or if I needed something fresh.

- **KIND.** There was constantly and consistently a spirit of kindness in all his actions.

And most importantly, Tom was always in my corner, win or lose, in and out of the ring. And he loved Old Spice cologne! That alone made him unforgettable.

It seemed so obvious. Why hadn't I connected Tom with everything I'd become and all the great work I was doing? Maybe I forgot about Tom because I was ashamed of not becoming a professional athlete and had pushed that life aside. Whatever the reason, I hadn't consciously realized the impact he had made in my life. The reason why didn't really matter now.

What mattered was the realization that his wisdom and influence is a major reason why I am who I am today and how I coach and help others realize their potential. Sadness immediately came over me when I realized I'd never told him. In that moment, I decided I needed to go back and let him know. I booked my flight and picked up the phone and called Tom. I'd had a few conversations with him over the years—just as friendly catch-ups. Whenever I called, he was always happy to hear from me. This time when I called, I shared with him that I was going to be in Chicago soon and wanted to stop by and see him.

A month later, I pulled up to his house. He lived a few minutes from O'Hare Airport just outside of Chicago. I remember the excitement and fear in preparation for this conversation. I had never really let anyone know how they had helped me when I needed help. I felt very vulnerable as I walked up to the door. It seemed more challenging than walking into the ring in front of thousands of people for my first televised championship fight for the Chicago Golden Gloves heavyweight title when I faced Oliver McCall, a future professional heavyweight champion of the world.

I walked into his home, and immediately Tom's Chihuahuas started barking and running all over the place, and Tom yelled out "Big Steve" and his wife, June, greeted me. It was like I'd seen them yesterday . . . I was home.

We sat out on the back porch. It was a warm, humid summer day, and we could hear the planes taking off and landing. We had a few sodas. Tom was a big drinker in the old days, but when the doc said no more drinking, it was sodas from then on.

We were out in the backyard for several hours talking and reminiscing about boxing and old times. Tom was very interested in what I was doing as a coach. He complimented me about how well I turned out and appreciated my coming by to spend some time with him. As our visit was coming to an end, I knew it was time to tell him what a positive influence he had on me. After all, that realization was what had inspired this trip, and there was no way I was leaving until I told him.

In the last few minutes of my visit, I said, "Hey, Tom, I just want to let you know how much I appreciate all your kindness, friendship, and guidance that you gave me from the first day I met you in the gym. It made a big impact on my life, and I'm just sorry I didn't tell you any sooner." Then there was silence.

I could tell he was caught off guard. The moment felt uncomfortable, and I could see that we were both feeling uneasy. A few moments later, which seemed like an eternity, he tried to deflect the attention from him. He said that it was his pleasure and that he was so proud of how I turned out and the work I was doing. He further explained that it was nothing, that I was already on the right path; he had just given me a little help.

That couldn't have been farther from the truth. I had needed all the help I could get back then.

After that, I went to visit Tom every year, and each year it got a little easier to show him my appreciation. And each year, he was a bit more comfortable accepting my appreciation. I could see as he got older how much he enjoyed our visits. The discomfort and vulnerability I initially felt was replaced with a deep feeling of connection and love, and I could see it was impacting him on a deeper level and me as well. Though I greatly valued my visits with Tom, I also went back to honor him and the legacy he created through me.

LESSONS LEARNED

Here are the lessons I learned from my time with Tom:

- Commit to the relationships that matter.
- Your why is the key to your existence.
- Time is always on your side when you take action.
- Be vulnerable.

- Your why can inspire courageous life-changing action.

- It's never too late to let people know what they mean to you and to honor them.

YOUR VALUES ARE WHERE YOU SPEND YOUR TIME

At the center of your being you have the answer;
you know who you are and you know what you want.
—Lao Tzu

Have you ever wondered why you are not where you want to be in your business or life, why you're not making the progress you feel you should, or why you're not as happy as you want to be? You are about to find out if your misaligned values are blocking your success.

A clear understanding and organization of your values provides direction—a road map of how you spend your time, money, and energy. Your values are what you believe in. They help you determine whether your actions are aligned with your why/purpose. Additionally, they help you decide how you feel about your actions as a representation of what's important to you.

Without an understanding of your values and what is most important, you become reactive and prone to making decisions based on your current day-to-day emotions. This is one of the major reasons that people make poor decisions, underperform, waste time, and drift off course. They are driven by their emotions and old programming rather than making a rational choice based on their values today.

To determine your values in any area of your life, ask yourself a simple question: "What is important to me in my life?" Words like "health," "happiness," "money," "security," "fun," "quality relationships," "love," "creativity," and "accomplishment" might be your values.

Below is a list of common values I have my clients and workshop participants use that can spark your thinking about your values. For now, just take a look at these to begin your thinking. There are hundreds of values, so don't be limited to the list.

Values

Family	Business	Health
Career	Spirituality	Creativity
Fun	Mindfulness	Giving
Integrity	Independence	Religion/God
Growth	Love	Legacy
Money	Happiness	Abundance
Security	Contribution	Significance
Serenity	Uniqueness	Peace
Service	Leadership	Grit
Kindness	Recognition	Freedom

To get you familiar with the values process, I want to share a great example I think will help you understand how valuable this exercise can be.

VALUES IN ACTION

I was working with one of my clients, Mark Macdonald, early in his career. Mark is a nutritionist and owner of Venice Nutrition, which was located at the famed Gold's Gym in Venice, California, known as the mecca of body building.

Mark is one of the most hardworking and caring guys I know. When I met him, he was already successful, working with top professional athletes, models, celebrities, executives, and other people who wanted to perform at their best, get in shape, and be fit and healthy. Now Mark wanted to take his program to the world and eradicate obesity. He was in the process of developing an online nutrition system, certification, and book and was, and continues to be, passionate and dedicated to helping people live in optimal health.

When we met, Mark told me, "I wake up at 4 a.m. every day and drive 1.5 hours to get to work. I work out, run my business, and see my clients; then I try to fit in time to work on expanding my business to take my nutrition system to a global platform. It's hard to find enough time because I need to leave work to avoid traffic, so I can spend quality hours with my wife." Mark was struggling to balance his personal life, his business, and his mission. Sound familiar?

As I listened further, I suggested we start by looking at his values and do a values alignment process. I explained to Mark that taking a look at his values would help him organize what was most important to him right now and how better to use his time in his life. I shared with him that when individuals are not getting the results they want out of life or with the speed they want, they are usually operating under the influence of conflicting values. That conflict can lead to a misalignment—a misplacement of where they invest their time and energy.

We started the process simply by writing a list on the whiteboard in his office. I asked him to make a list in the order of what was most important to him and his life.

Mark wrote:

1. Family/wife

2. Business

3. Health

4. Integrity

5. Travel

As he wrote them down, I talked through each one to gain clarity of what each meant to him. Now, for the record, when a person does this for the first time, it can be challenging, because most people haven't really listed their values in a sequence that suggests priority.

After talking through each, I then said, "I see Abbi, your wife, is first."

"Yes," he replied, "my wife is my first priority. Abbi is my everything."

Then I asked this test question: "If your business is failing or not growing because you are not putting enough time into it, as long as you have a good relationship with your wife, is that OK?"

Without hesitation he said: "No, that would be horrible. I wouldn't be fulfilling my life purpose or be able to satisfy my financial obligations."

I told him, "You have a values conflict. I know your wife is very important; however, if you put your wife before your business, you are going to be deeply unhappy, and she is not going to feel very good either."

I instructed Mark to rearrange the order on the whiteboard putting business first, and then he took a step back. And before I could continue, he said, "I already know what has to be first, 'integrity'; without that, nothing matters," and he placed that first.

Then I asked, "If your relationship is good with your wife, but you're not taking care of your health, would that be OK?"

Once again, he immediately said, "No, I have to be healthy to be the best I can be for her." He then reordered the list again.

His new alignment was the following:

1. Integrity

2. Health

3. Business

4. Family/wife

5. Travel

We went through the list one more time to check that the order reflected his true priorities. As he looked at his values on the board, his face suddenly shifted from excitement to worry. I asked what was going on for him as I saw the shift, and he said, "I can't go home and tell my wife she is number four on my values list. She will divorce me!"

I then said, "Mark, here's the thing. You have been operating in a blind spot in how your values were arranged based on past programing that was keeping you from advancing at the level you wanted. You've been making decisions about where you're putting your time, focus, and energy that do not support your vision. Now that you really understand what's important to you and why, you can begin to see that how and where you spend your *time* is determining whether you succeed or fail in living your values. That's why you are struggling.

"Mark, when your integrity, your health, and your business are aligned, your wife will feel like she's number one. If not, you'll continue to struggle, and she will not feel like she is number one."

Mark went home that night and shared his revelation with Abbi, and she totally understood. In fact, she was 100 percent on board. She could see that by living his values and reorienting his time, Mark could live with more ease and use his energy, passion, and focus to invest in their relationship and all that mattered to the two of them.

From that moment on, struggle gave way to opportunity, and Mark accelerated his business faster than ever before by prioritizing his time and reorganizing his schedule in a way that reflected his values. He could now expand time to all that was important to him.

Now their family has grown to include two beautiful children, and Mark is more deeply connected with his wife and kids than ever. His business has expanded to thousands of nutritionists certified in his program, and he has his own nutritional product line, is a regular contributor on CNN, has a wellness segment on the HLN network, and is a *New York Times* bestselling author! Realigning his values *focused* his time and energy in the right places, and he created the life of his dreams.

DETERMINING YOUR VALUES

Follow the steps below to determine your life values:

1. Ask yourself this question: "What is most important to me in my life?" Use the list of values that follow as a starting point, and circle the 10 that are most important to you. You can also add any that aren't on the list, but be sure you are circling what *you* value, not what you or someone else thinks you should value.

VALUES		
Family	Business	Health
Career	Spirituality	Creativity
Fun	Mindfulness	Giving
Integrity	Independence	Religion/God
Growth	Love	Legacy
Money	Happiness	Abundance
Security	Contribution	Significance
Serenity	Uniqueness	Peace
Service	Leadership	Grit
Kindness	Recognition	Freedom

2. Now take a hard look at the 10 values you selected. Think about which of these are most important to you, and identify your top five.

> Values question: "What is most important to me in my life?"
>
> 1. _____
>
> 2. _____
>
> 3. _____
>
> 4. _____
>
> 5. _____

3. Now that you've identified your top five values, think about the order in which they should be listed. My list looks like this:

   1. Health
   2. Business
   3. Fun
   4. Friends/family
   5. Being of service

   To make sure they are in the correct order, ask yourself, "If I could have my number one value, *not* my number two value, would that be OK?" If the answer is yes, then the order is correct. However, if your answer is no, then swap accordingly. Continue this process for all five values until your order is clear and established.

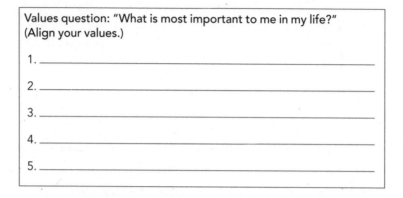

Values question: "What is most important to me in my life?"
(Align your values.)

1. _____

2. _____

3. _____

4. _____

5. _____

You may find you have to really take some time to think about the answers. By doing this, you are accessing some very valuable information. Take note of how you feel about each comparison as you apply the question to each of them. Notice which choices are particularly difficult. It's possible you may go back and forth a few times switching your answers. This is totally normal and part of the process.

Your results might shock you. Perhaps some of the values you thought were important to you are not actually as high up on your list as you initially considered them. That's OK! This just means that while some things (like friendships) may be very important, others (like family) take priority.

This process of aligning your values allows you to reveal what is most important to you in any area of your life (your business or career, relationships, health and fitness, etc.) for where you are now and where you want to be. We're going to be using them as a guide throughout the Time Cleanse process.

CHECK YOUR ALIGNMENT

Now that you have established your top five values in order, let's do a quick check-in to see that your values are aligned and correctly aligned with your why.

Review your values list and ask yourself the following questions:

1. "Are my values aligned to whom I need to be to have what I want in life?"

2. "Do I need to add any other values to the list to be aligned or eliminate any that will keep me from being the person I need to be to have what I most want?"

3. "Do I feel that these five values are in alignment with my why?"

After reviewing, make any adjustments if needed.

Aligning your values with your why is critical, because if your values are off, you will be making decisions that create conflict and roadblocks that slow your progress and keep you from realizing your full potential.

One more thing: Be aware that even though your values are complete, it's a good idea to review them every quarter to see if any of your values need to be realigned with your current priorities. Values can shift and change as you change over time.

Now let's take what we've done so far and turn that into tangible goals for what you want.

GOALS AND INTENTIONS WITH TIME

> What keeps me going is goals.
> —MUHAMMAD ALI

Now it's time to let your why and the values you've just established guide you in mapping out your goals and intentions.

Goals

A goal is a desired outcome you want to achieve that is *future* oriented with *time*. Goals set the mark to know exactly what you want to obtain. For many people, goals on their own can feel distant and even unreachable in any given moment. That is where intention connects our will and attention with goals that keep us on a path moving forward.

Intentions

Intention is a mindset that is *present* oriented with *time*. Intentions allow you to focus your time now on how you want to be in this moment. They guide your actions, energy, and focus on what matters most to you. They can easily be created and renewed daily, keeping you directed toward your goals. Intentions bring you fully into the moment each day. They raise your emotional energy, which in turn raises your physical energy, allowing you to accomplish more. Aligned intention makes it possible to consistently live from your values and purpose as you take actions toward your goals.

NYU researchers Peter Gollwitzer and Veronika Brandstatter discovered the power of intentions. In their research, they found that people who set intentions, even when vague, can increase their success rate by 20 percent.[2] And when intentions are set with specific details, those success rates can double or even triple! That is a powerful argument to set your daily intentions.

Comparing the Two

Let's look at how goals and intentions work together.

A simple way to think about setting up your intention is to make sure you include the behavior, time, and location:

- **GOAL.** I will increase my sales 20 percent this quarter.
- **GENERAL INTENTION.** I will be present in the moment, so I can be responsive to client questions and maximize today's opportunities.
- **SPECIFIC INTENTION.** In each of my eight meetings today, I will be present in the moment and responsive—moving the sales process forward.

- **GOAL.** I will lose 10 pounds this month.
- **GENERAL INTENTION.** I will make smart eating choices that I have predetermined for the day.

- **SPECIFIC INTENTION.** I will bring to work today my premade meals to eat every four hours.

- **GOAL.** I will become a better team leader this year.
- **GENERAL INTENTION.** I will actively listen with patience today.
- **SPECIFIC INTENTION.** I will coach my sales team today with patience and good listening skills and create a supportive work environment.

Setting *specific* intentions is a powerful way of directing your conscious energy, attention, and time toward your future goals.

Setting Goals

We set goals for one simple reason: to know what the destination is so we can direct our time, energy, and focus to achieve them. Our intentions help us get there as fast as possible while enjoying the process. When determining your goals, they should feel a bit or a lot out of your comfort zone, even to the edge of what you think is possible. This a very individual process. The important thing to remember here is to get out of your comfort zone but not to the point you are overwhelmed.

You can begin the process by asking yourself these questions:

Goal-Setting Questions to Get You Focused on Your Goals

1. "What is my goal or desired outcome?"
2. "Where am I today?"
3. "What resources do I already have? What resources do I need (people/things)?"
4. "What is the time frame?"

Setting SMART Goals Through the Lens of Time

SMART means the goal must be *S*pecific, *M*easurable, *A*ttainable, *R*elevant, and *T*ime-centered.

- **SPECIFIC.** Create your goal with as much detail as possible. It should be written with precision, clarity, and specifics focusing on the Five Ws.

  Questions to ask: who, what, where, when, and why?

- **MEASURABLE.** Establish specific criteria for measuring your goal so you can track your progress and stay motivated.

  Questions to ask: "How will I know when it is accomplished?" "How much?" "How many?" This will give you the details for how to measure it—for example, in income, pounds lost, hours saved, etc.

- **ATTAINABLE.** Make sure your goal is achievable and realistic; it should stretch you and still be obtainable.

  Questions to ask: "What appropriate and inspired actions do I need to take to meet my goal?" "How can I achieve this goal?"

- **RELEVANT.** Choose a goal that you are both *willing* and *able* to put the appropriate time and effort into and that actually matters to you and/or the collective.

  Questions to ask: "Does it connect to my overall short- and long-term plans?" "Is this goal going to make a positive difference for me and/or others?" "Is this aligned with my why or purpose, and my values?"

- **TIME-CENTERED.** Have scheduled and trackable tasks and timelines. This inspires action and holds you accountable. Set a specific time frame for accomplishing your goal.

  Questions to ask: "When will this goal be completed?" "Am I committed to investing the time needed?"

Here are some example responses:

- "I will increase my sales by 30 percent by obtaining 10 or more new clients by the end of the year, selling our new subscription program."

- "I will lose 10 pounds within the next three months, going to the gym five times a week for an hour and eating balanced meals every four hours."

- "I will complete my beginner's Japanese language course this month listening to one lesson a day for 30 minutes."

Research shows that having goals is important, but writing them down significantly improves your success rate.

A study by Dr. Gail Matthews at Dominican University in California looked at the science of goal setting by tracking 267 people—men and women from all over the world and from all walks of life, including entrepreneurs, educators, healthcare professionals, artists, lawyers, and bankers.

She split them into two groups, one that wrote down their goals and one that did not. Those who wrote down their goals had a 42 percent increase in goal achievement compared with those who didn't.[3]

SETTING GOALS WORKSHEET

Now that you know how important it is to write your goals down, write out your specific goals for the following areas. They can be for the year, the quarter, or the month, whatever best fits your specific needs. And if there are any other areas in which you want to set goals for yourself that are not listed, please do add them! You can download this worksheet at www.timecleanse.com/book.

YOUR TOP THREE GOALS

Career

1. _____
2. _____
3. _____

Finances

1. _____
2. _____
3. _____

Health and Fitness

1. _____
2. _____
3. _____

Relationships

1. _____
2. _____
3. _____

Becoming (who you want to be or more of)

1. _____
2. _____
3. _____

You've now established what you're committed to and why, aligned your values, and written out specific goals that are important to you.

In this chapter, you've covered a lot of ground by identifying many goals that are truly important to you. To get the most out of the Time Cleanse, use your goals as a guide to determine what's most important to you now. By doing so, you'll successfully reclaim the greatest number of hours for what matters the most in your life.

4

Time Toxins

Time is the coin of your life. It is the only coin you have,
and only you can determine how it will be spent.
Be careful lest you let other people spend it for you.
—CARL SANDBURG

A "TIME TOXIN" IS ANY BEHAVIOR, ACTIVITY, HABIT, person, place, or thing that consumes, steals, hijacks, or contaminates your time and causes you to become stuck, stalled, or stopped when working toward achieving what matters most to you. And this is a crucial part of the Time Cleanse. You need to begin identifying and eliminating these toxins to create more time for those things that matter most to you.

THE BIG COST OF SMALL TOXINS

In the mid-1990s, a famous researcher, Karen Wetterhahn, accidentally dropped a few seemingly inconsequential milliliters of the deadly compound dimethyl mercury on her double-gloved hand while engaged in research. Over the course of several months, she began experiencing problems with balance and speech. After months of not understanding why she wasn't feeling well, she went to the emergency room. A blood test revealed she was suffering from mercury poisoning.

It turned out that the latex gloves she had worn were not resistant to the form of mercury she used. Instead, it seeped through the glove and was absorbed into her skin. Unlike most cases of mercury poisoning, she wasn't exposed over the course of months or years; it was just one incident. It's reported that it was about an hour before she realized the chemical had soaked through the glove—and that one hour set her fate.

Sadly, the mercury damaged her brain and eventually her whole nervous system, and less than six months later she died from the complications of those few drops of mercury.[1]

While not nearly as devastating as this story, there are things in your life that are toxic, are stealing your time, and are causing you damage. These toxins, even small ones, can have a big, devastating, fast, and long-lasting effect without your even realizing it.

Let's take a look at some common time toxins that may be hijacking your life:

1. **SOCIAL MEDIA.** You are spending an hour on Facebook or other social media when you are bored or stressed.

2. **GOSSIP.** You are spending an extra 20 minutes a day gossiping and talking at the coffee shop.

3. **TELEVISION-ONLINE MOVIES.** You've developed a longtime habit of watching endless television at night, and now that you can stream almost anything, anytime, you can binge-watch 24/7.

4. **NEGATIVE PEOPLE.** While you used to enjoy time spent with an old friend, he is disenchanted with life and complains every time you talk.

5. **OVERWORK.** Increased demands at work have pushed your sales calls to the end of the day when you're tired and fatigued. While the effort is still being made, the timing is off for your best performance.

6. **THE NEWS.** The changing world has made you a news junkie, and your newsfeed constantly interrupts your day, as the more news you hear, the more you feel the need to know.

7. **TEXTING.** What started as a small way to stay connected with friends has now become a constant distraction—even at work.

8. **YOUR PHONE.** You're repeatedly reaching for your phone when you're bored and to serve as a distraction when you could be productive instead.

9. **SHOPPING.** You're spending endless hours looking at, comparing, and researching things you want to buy.

10. **MULTITASKING.** You're moving from one task to the next, which results in your not being fully present to produce quality and effective work.

As you begin to become aware of these toxins more and more, it's important to remember that it's not your fault that toxins have made their way into your life. This is something that happens to each of us and has become a natural part of how we live today. However, now that you're aware that they exist, you can stop them and eliminate them from entering your life at all.

To begin removing time toxins from your life, you'll need to start evaluating where you're spending your time. Once you have identified something as a potential toxin, it's time to ask the Time Cleanse Question:

> "Is this contributing or contaminating
> to my happiness and success?"

This is the Time Cleanse question that will provide immediate clarity, showing what is supporting you or what may be holding you back from getting what matters most in your life and achieving your full potential. No matter what you come across, if it's a *behavior, activity, habit, person, place, or thing*, the answer to this question will give you insight into how to use your time. As you move through the rest of this book, the Time Cleanse question will be your guide to instant clarity with your time in every situation.

CONTRIBUTING OR CONTAMINATING?

Contributing

Let's start with *contributing*. The following are questions to ask yourself that can help you get a clear sense if *behaviors, activities, habits, people, places, or things* are contributing value to your life. Consider the following mental and emotional states that indicate contribution.

As an example, let's use social media, such as Facebook, or even a friend in your life:

Ask yourself: Does this . . .

- Inspire me or motivate me?

- Bring me joy?

- Move me closer to my goal?

- Create enthusiasm, connection, or engagement for me?

- Bring out my best?

- Connect me with something larger than myself?

- Bring relevance and make me feel like I'm making a difference?

Contaminating

Now let's take a look at *contaminating*.

Ask yourself: Does this . . .

- Drain or exhaust me?

- Frustrate or distract me?

- Anger or agitate me?

- Cause resistance in me?

- Stifle, put down, or demean me?

- Block or hold me back?

TIME AND TIMING

An additional factor to consider when deciding whether something is contributing or contaminating to your happiness and success is the amount of time you're engaged with it and/or the timing of it.

1. **TIME DURATION.** "Is this the optimal amount of time to engage in what I'm doing for maximum productivity?" For example, Facebook for 15 minutes may be something that is contributing, but when it's an hour or two, it becomes a contaminant.

2. **TIME OF DAY.** "What's the best time during the day to engage in what I'm doing?" Being on Facebook while also being on a weekly business conference call may be contaminating, but engaging in Facebook at home in your free time may be a positive contributor to your social life.

I've taught the Time Cleanse to thousands of people, in hundreds of workshops, and when presenting the Time Cleanse Question, time and time again it proves that when we stop and become present in what we are doing, we actually intuitively know if something is contributing or contaminating to our happiness and success.

Of course, everything in life is not absolute, and there will be degrees of each, but I ask you to determine if something is contributing or contaminating. There is a fine line, and you know the answer, even if you've not considered it before.

What's important now is to bring attention and awareness to your time toxins and consider their impact. You may have never been taught the proper process to accurately evaluate how, when, where, and with whom you spend your time. Many of your behaviors have been embedded for so long that now they are unconscious habits that continue even though they no longer have value or purpose. I often ask clients when I take them through the Time Cleanse why they are still engaged in a particular behavior. The most frequent response I get is, "I never stopped to think about it . . . I've just always done it that way." They usually have a look of shock at first and then relief when they begin to realize it's a toxin they can change right now or remove it.

Traps

Traps are the mental and emotional patterns we get caught in that over time can be how toxins come to live and stay in our lives. Here are the four big ones:

1. Explaining why.

2. Pretending not to know.

3. Someday.

4. I've always done it this way.

Let's take a look at each one so you have an understanding of how they work and how to overcome them.

Explaining Why

When I work with clients, I find that many people want to defend *why* they are spending their time in certain ways. Many times, they believe that the problem and solution lie outside of them. Their argument becomes focused on the situation, person, or behavior versus the choice, control, and power they themselves have in controlling the issue. They get caught up in the symptoms and circumstances of "It will never change" or "I can't change it," believing they are powerless, which then feeds the loop of their "why" conversation. They act like a victim, losing sight of and disconnecting from the fact that they can actually shift, remove, or resolve the issue.

This is a normal defense mechanism against change but has absolutely no bearing on whether any item contributes or contaminates. What is important here is breaking the cycle of explaining why and deciding whether a certain *behavior, activity, habit, person, place, or thing* is holding you back or is moving you toward your goals and who you want to be.

Pretending Not to Know

Another common trap is pretending not to know, which happens when people convince themselves that a person, behavior, habit, or thing is not toxic and therefore not adversely affecting them.

Our constant busyness and distractions set up a lack of awareness around what is really going on in our lives. This creates a condition of not being present and pretending not to know what's actually going on.

To counteract this trap, ask the following question:

"What am I pretending not to know?"

Let's look at this question in action:

"What am I pretending not to know about my friend Jonathan and my interactions with him?"

Answer: "I am pretending not to know Johnathan is very negative about everything in life, and when I am around him, it brings my energy down and makes me feel like nothing ever works out."

Taking the time to ask this question will provide insight if something is contributing or contaminating to your happiness and success.

Someday

A third trap my clients fall into is "someday." Here, clients tend to use the following statement to justify why they aren't achieving their goals:

When (this happens) _____, then I can _____.

FOR EXAMPLE:

- "When I balance my life, then I can be healthy and fit."

- "When I lose 20 pounds, then I can have the relationship of my dreams."

- "When my kids turn 18, then I can start living my life again."

- "When the economy changes, then I can be successful."

This trap is a stalling technique that tricks your mind into thinking you aren't ready and that success is dependent on some outside factor. To break away from this trap, you have to shift your mindset from "Why I can't" to "How I can."

In reality, you have to first make a decision that you want something with full conviction. This will force your mind to find a way to create the time for it. It *never* happens in reverse. That's why people stay stuck. You must seek the information, knowledge, wisdom, or coaching to make it happen.

To break free from this trap, ask yourself, "If I did (blank) right now, how would my life be enhanced? If I took one small or big step right now toward what I want, what would change or be set in motion?"

I've Always Done It This Way

The fourth trap is all about habits and routines. We can all become creatures of habit in which our brains become trained to do things on autopilot. This trap is an easy one to be stuck in because you no longer *consciously think* about what you are doing, and things happen outside of your consciousness.

The brain loves habits—both good and bad—because it no longer has to think. The reason the Time Cleanse is so transforming is that it encourages people to consciously stop and ask, "Is this contributing or contaminating to my happiness and success?" The solution to breaking this trap is to ask the question, "How could I do it differently?"

Once you've asked these questions, your critical thinking will kick in and awaken you to new possibilities and choices.

THE TIME HANGOVER EFFECT

All these toxins and traps can cause a "time hangover." When you have too many toxins in your body, like too much alcohol, you experience a hangover and feel bad for an extended period of time. The time you spend feeling bad is much longer than the time you spent "enjoying" the toxic activity. Toxic activities, it turns out, are very bad investments—you pay the price the next day, and possibly for many weeks, months, and even years to come. *The time hangover effect is the unexpected cost of your lost time and performance in the future.*

For example, if you need to prepare for an early morning meeting, but you decide to take a break and watch your favorite Netflix series, suddenly one episode turns into four hours of binge-watching. Not only are you now unprepared for the meeting the next day, but you're also in a sleep deficit with far less energy and much more stress. That sleep deficit could have an effect on you for the entire week, all from one toxic activity.

I had one client whose major time toxin turned out to be the coffee shop across the street. A simple 10-minute coffee break would turn into hours per week of conversations with familiar people and friends that ate up his most productive afternoon work time. You can't recover your prime-time work hours. You can't make sales calls at 11 p.m. Those lost hours had a much bigger impact than just the hours spent in the coffee shop. They slowed down his entire business, as if he'd been going to work with a hangover every day. When he removed the time toxin, his entire life and performance changed.

Wasting time with a *behavior, activity, habit, person, place, or thing* that upsets you, or makes you frustrated throughout your day, creates a time hangover. It ends up lowering your productivity, draining your energy, and hurting your performance.

I've Always Done It This Way

I was born and raised in Chicago, and the early days were not easy. My mom raised me and my younger brother basically on her own. We lived in a small apartment in a lower-income neighborhood on and off government assistance and food stamps. My mom did an awesome job under the circumstances with what we had, but I knew at an early age that this wasn't the life I wanted for me and my family. I was willing to do whatever it took to change my circumstances.

At 13 years old, the only way I could see out was through athletics. So even though I was tall and skinny, I committed myself to football and decided that I was going to get a football scholarship and someday make it to the NFL. This wasn't my dream—it was my plan. This goal became my entire life; every waking minute was dedicated to becoming an elite athlete.

I dedicated myself to football while in high school and worked hard. My talent was obvious, but there weren't any Division I scouts knocking on my door. At 6 feet 4 inches and 170 pounds, I knew I had to bulk up in order to play at the next level. Failure was not an option. So I enrolled in a local junior college. I researched and sought out everything I could to get bigger, faster, and stronger. With complete focus and commitment, two years later and in my sophomore year in junior college, I was 6 feet 5 inches and 230 pounds and began getting noticed as a tight end by college scouts who were filling the stands on a weekly basis.

In the fifth game that season, I tore my hamstring while making a spectacular catch. Lying face down on the field while excruciating pain was shooting down my leg, I automatically went to the worst possible scenario; my dream of getting a scholarship and being a professional athlete ended in a heartbeat. At that moment, I felt like my life was over.

But I was determined to take charge of my own future. I began rehabbing immediately, and five weeks later I was as back to 80 percent—good enough to play in our last game of the season, the championship. I was taped from my waist down to my ankle to protect my hamstring. I made it through the game, and a few weeks later Western Michigan offered me a Division I scholarship to play football. It wasn't one of the Big Ten powerhouses like Michigan or Ohio State that I had set my sights on, but it was a good school and an awesome opportunity. Most importantly, it was progress and it was a step higher on my ladder to success. I was extremely excited to put on those shoulder pads and take the field for that first practice, just raring to go and make a great impression.

But shortly into the beginning of the first spring practice at Western Michigan, I experienced the same nightmare all over again. I tore the same hamstring on a simple outpost route. And it felt like the world had ended. Again.

Now remember, there's a ticking clock on eligibility for college football, and I had already wasted two years with two different hamstring injuries. I started looking at NAIA (National Association of Intercollegiate Athletics) schools that would extend my eligibility because of different guidelines, at least to finish out the next year or two. I decided on Mesa College in Grand Junction, Colorado. The team had a very broad group of players, and the school was willing to give me a scholarship. They had troubled players who'd washed out of Division I schools because of grades, drugs or run-ins with the police, plus a few athletes like me who were trying to overcome injuries and salvage their careers. And here's the thing: Every year, some of the guys got free agent shots, and some actually made it to the NFL. So I still had hope of making it.

If I finished my first season at Mesa, even though I still wasn't 100 percent, I could use the upcoming off-season to push myself harder than ever to get back to 100 percent. And I did just that. I showed up that next fall in the best shape of my life at 250 pounds. I felt massive, powerful, and absolutely unstoppable.

Seniors had the opportunity to do a number of tests for visiting pro scouts. And I thought, this was my big chance to blow these guys away and show them what kind of athlete I really was. So when I stepped up to the line to run the 40-yard dash, I pushed myself harder than I ever had before.

I was flying down the track and put up my fastest 40-yard time ever, tumbling onto the track as I crossed the finish line. I had just torn my other hamstring. I lay there feeling the hot asphalt on my skin, screaming inside my head, "I can't believe it's happened again!"

With my third hamstring injury, it doesn't take a genius to see that this was a pattern. No matter how hard I worked, it seemed I wasn't going to make it. I was beyond devastated. Since the age of 13, I had one goal in life—to play football in the NFL. It was my ticket to the successful life I desperately wanted. I couldn't even imagine a life where I wasn't working for that. The truth is, I had such low self-esteem that I believed football was the only thing I could ever be good at and without that I was worthless. So, I kept pushing forward.

Unable to play that season, I began rehabbing again and decided I couldn't give up. In my mind, I had no choice. I committed to pushing harder than ever before over that summer and doing everything possible to be successful. I trained twice a day and ate everything in sight, bulked up to nearly 300 pounds, and once again felt indestructible.

The following season, I returned to college ready to take on anything in my path. In training camp with my size, the coach moved me to tackle, and I was performing really well. I loved it; I was dominating at my new position on the field.

But then something happened. I woke up on a Saturday morning about a week into camp and realized I didn't want to go to practice. I wasn't tired or sore or anything like that; I just didn't want to go. In fact, I never wanted to go to practice again.

In a moment of complete clarity, I realized my passion for football was gone. Just like that. It was as if something in my mind had snapped into place to give me this one piece of clarity. I actually lay there laughing, because at 24 years old and 300 pounds, I was living my life by my 13-year-old mindset. I clearly saw, for the first time, that the only thing I really ever wanted to do was be successful. What was keeping me going in this direction after all these injuries was that I didn't want to fail—yet I was failing myself.

Three schools, three coaches, three injuries. Time had changed things, but I hadn't changed. Time had passed me by, but *I* was still living in the past. I had kept climbing the ladder of success, one step at a time, only to find out that morning *that the ladder was leaning against the wrong wall.*

As I lay there in bed, I knew success was now going to take on another dimension, something different that I would love. I gathered all my gear and went to the head football coach's office, met with him, and laid the equipment on his desk. And as soon as the gear left my hands, I felt an immediate release from the mental prison I'd locked myself in. Unbelievable joy, happiness, and relief overtook me. There was finally room for a whole new future.

That decision released the belief I had programmed into myself that I could only be successful through football. Although that had served me well years earlier, I knew in that moment that my narrow thinking and limited beliefs were the exact things holding me back.

The thing that is crystal clear to me today is that I was so conditioned and hypnotized on autopilot that I never once stopped to evaluate if this was still the right course. I had just always done it this way. By stopping to evaluate, I realized I actually had a choice in the matter. I was stuck in a toxic trap that I'd created, causing myself a tremendous amount of pain and suffering that I didn't need to endure. I was now free to pursue success in something new.

The question I have for you is this: What contaminant, toxic trap, or "blind spot" is holding you back? What's currently in your life that you're spending time, energy, and effort on that you need to let go of? Perhaps you need a course correction so you're not wasting time on things that don't really matter anymore. Maybe you're still operating with old ideas that need to be released.

Now it's your time to cleanse yourself of what's no longer serving you today.

Blind Spots

> We must be willing to get rid of the life we've planned,
> so as to have the life that is waiting for us.
> —Joseph Campbell

In my years of coaching I've learned that women and men at every level in all fields have "hidden roadblocks" that keep them stuck and struggling when it comes to time and its relationship to achievement, success, and performance. I call these "blind spots."

What Are Blind Spots?

Blind spots are a protective mechanism of your subconscious mind to stop you from seeing your limiting beliefs and to keep you "safe" and comfortable and on the familiar road. But the familiar road is also keeping you from realizing your full potential. Blind spots are usually programming from our past or from specific life events along the way.

Traditionally, the term "blind spot" is used to refer to an area you are not able to see in your car's rearview or side view mirror while you are driving. When you need to switch lanes, out of habit you glance in the rearview mirror and the mirror on the driver's side door, and then you physically turn your head around and glance at the blind spot that the mirrors can't cover.

Outside of driving, blind spots have conditioned us to think in a limiting and nonresourceful way. These blind spots result in underperformance in our careers, finances, relationships, and health and wellness. Because you're stuck in an environment where you cannot see what is potentially damaging, you cannot change what you cannot see—until now.

The Time Cleanse not only reveals your blind spots and limiting beliefs, it compels you to examine them and then offers a process to release what has been holding you back.

The Two Types of Blind Spots

In my work with the thousands of people who have participated in the Time Cleanse, I have identified two types of blind spots:

1. **BEHAVIOR.** This is something you are doing that you're not aware of being a toxin. It might be the *amount* of time you're spending on something or even the time of the day that makes it toxic (e.g., going on Facebook for one hour a day or stopping at the coffee shop daily for 30 minutes).

2. **BELIEF.** This is something more deeply rooted in your subconscious, a belief you're not aware of. As a result, you can't seem to take appropriate action to shift or change this behavior, habit, or thing that is toxic in your life. A common comment clients say to me when this is happening is "I don't know why I keep doing (x). I know I shouldn't, but I can't seem to help myself."

Now, let's take a look at how you can break through your blind spots.

Breaking Through Your Blind Spots

> Whether you think you can,
> or you think you can't—you're right.
> —HENRY FORD

The fastest way to break through limiting beliefs is to ask yourself one question:

"Who do I need to be to have what I want?"

You can ask yourself this question about any area of your life where you desire a breakthrough. You can also use this if you notice a performance gap, such as in your career, finances, relationships, health and wellness, etc.

By following the steps below, you will see how you can uncover the limiting beliefs that may be holding you back. This process is available for download at www.timecleanse.com/book.

STEP 1. Define specifically what it is you want.

_____

STEP 2. Answer the question, "Who do I need to be to have what I want?"

_____

STEP 3. Answer the question, "What belief am I holding onto about myself that keeps me from being _____ (fill in the answer from Step 2)?"

_____

STEP 4. Answer the question, "What belief am I holding onto about myself that makes my answer to Step 3 true?"

_____

STEP 5. Repeat the question from Step 4 until you begin to recycle similar answers and intuitively feel you have reached your core answer.

_____

_____

_____

STEP 6. Once you have reached your core answer, ask yourself, "Is this answer or belief really true?"

If you answered yes, ask yourself, "Am I 100 percent sure this answer or belief is true?" and "Is it true 100 percent of the time?"

When you've answered no, you're done with the blind spot process. You can then move on to transforming your blind spot into an empowering belief process.

Next you'll see these prompts in action with one of my clients who was stuck in his career, struggling financially, and trying to get to his next level:

STEP 1. Define specifically what it is I want.
Answer: "I want to advance in my career and make more money."

STEP 2. "Who do I need to be to have what I want?"
Answer: "I need to be a more confident and assertive person in business."

STEP 3. "What belief am I holding onto about myself that keeps me from being 'confident and assertive'?"
Answer: "I don't have the right education."

STEPS 4–5. "What belief am I holding onto about myself that makes this true?"
Answer: "I'm not smart enough."

"What belief am I holding onto about myself that makes that true?"
Answer: "I don't have as much experience as others."

"What belief am I holding onto about myself that makes that true?"
Answer: "I'm not good enough."

"What belief am I holding onto about myself that makes that true?"
Answer: "I'm not good enough."

At this point, my client sensed he'd discovered his subconscious belief after he repeated "I'm not good enough."

Then, with Step 6, my client asked himself, "Am I 100 percent sure this belief is true?" ("I'm not good enough.") and "Is it true 100 percent of the time?"

His answer was a resounding and proud no.

The thousands of clients I have taken through this blind spot process have all eventually recognized that these old limiting beliefs are things we made up in our own minds. Uncovering them and then shifting them to an empowering belief is the key to activating your full potential.

Transforming Your Blind Spot into an Empowering Belief

Now that you have identified a blind spot that might be holding you back, it's time to shift your mindset to a powerful intention statement. The quickest and most powerful tool is to visualize exactly what you want as if you have already attained it.

While visualizing what you want, picture yourself having completed that goal. After a minute or so, ask yourself, "What belief allowed me to achieve this goal and supported me in making it a reality?" Your answer could be anything from "I am assertive and confident in my career" to "I have the wisdom to make the right decisions." It could also be "I have what it takes to complete any project," "I'm capable of being in a healthy, loving relationship," or a simple "I deserve to be happy."

Now that you've determined your new empowering belief and are focusing on it, write it down and use it as a daily intention to motivate you into taking action.

Outwitting the Devil

One of my favorite books was written over 80 years ago by an author named Napoleon Hill. It's a book called *Outwitting the Devil*.[2] Believe it or not, Napoleon Hill was too afraid to publish it at the time because he was worried how people would react. So he kept it on his shelf, and it wasn't discovered until after Napoleon passed away. And after years of debate, his family finally decided to publish it in his name.

In the book, Napoleon sat down to meet the devil face-to-face. It was implied that no matter what Napoleon asked, the devil had to tell the truth. Napoleon asked, "How do you get people to do what you want?"

The devil hesitated because he wasn't sure if he could give away such a big secret. After a short pause, he said, "You see, people don't think for themselves. Ninety-nine out of one hundred people just don't bother to think for themselves. So, it's easy to get them drifting off course doing what I want them to do."

Napoleon then said, "But how do you do this? How do you actually do it?" Again, the devil refused to answer, but Napoleon reminded him, "You promised, you promised to tell me the truth."

The devil replied, "I know exactly what each person needs to get off course. I know your weakness. For some, it might be sex, drugs, or over-eating. For others, it could be shopping or working too much. Once I get a person drifting off course, I have them. They enter into a hypnotic trance focusing on what I want. From there, I can make them do anything I want. They are powerless."

Napoleon then said, "Well, how can people outwit you then? How can they avoid falling into your trance?"

Well, the devil obviously didn't want to answer . . . but he had to. So after a little bit of stalling, he eventually said, "You just have to start thinking for yourself. The most important thing is to have a purpose in life. Once you focus on that one thing and commit to it, then I can't touch you anymore. It makes you invincible to me."

This story perfectly captures the idea that whenever you're not focused on what really matters in your life, you can become susceptible to toxins and contaminating distractions, and lost and going in the wrong direction on the wrong road.

The devil in this story is anything that isn't serving your larger purpose. And the scary truth is that modern society itself has become "its own sort of devil."

TIME CLEANSE IN ACTION: JAMES' STORY

I recently worked with James, a marketing and branding consultant in his mid-thirties who told me he always felt strapped for time. His goal was to launch a new online program for his marketing clients, and finding time to get it done was frustrating him. He was already spending dozens of hours on it, in addition to working with his regular full-time schedule. Not only did he use statements that felt constricting like "I never have enough time" or "I feel like the clock has a hold of me and I am powerless," but when he described his relationship with time, I could also see the tension in his face and body.

As I evaluated everything James shared with me, it became apparent that he had a major blind spot operating underneath his time issues. I had a good hunch what it was, but I relied on my blind spot process to reveal the truth.

We started with his specific goal: completing his online program.

When I asked, "Who do you need to be to have what you want [completing his online program]?" he answered, "I have to be in charge of my time."

When I asked, "What belief are you holding onto about yourself that keeps you from that?" he answered, "That time is working against me—that I never have enough time."

Then he said the following:

"I'm not good with time."

"I'm not disciplined."

"I'm not strong enough."

"I'm not deserving of it."

"I'm not smart enough."

"It has to be perfect."

"I'm not deserving of it."

Once he admitted each of these things and repeated "I'm not deserving of it," I realized he'd reached his core limiting belief.

I asked him, "Do you consciously believe any of that?"

James nearly jumped out of his chair confidently exclaiming "No!"

He consciously knew that wasn't true. Together, we discovered he had a blind spot hiding his old, deep limiting belief that he didn't deserve this kind of success if he didn't struggle to get it. Because of this belief, he kept struggling and spending extra time trying to make his online program "perfect."

Once he shifted his belief and realized that he didn't have to struggle and deserved success, things rapidly started to shift for him. He was focused, used his time effectively, and made remarkable progress on his online program. The internal stress and anxiety he had experienced were now visibly gone. He now was performing with time instead of fighting with it, as he previously had been doing.

As we worked through the Time Cleanse further, I showed him a new way to understand how he chose to use his time, and he began to uncover contaminants. He realized he was misusing and misjudging the amount of time he was online, especially when viewing news sites and engaging in social media. He thought he was spending a few minutes to recharge and relax, but instead discovered he was actually spending several hours a day.

As James began to keep track of his online habits, he discovered he could reclaim 7 hours a week by reducing his online news consumption and 3 more hours a week simply by cutting back on his non-business-related social media use. As he continued to evaluate the other areas of his time use, just like that, James, who was chronically unable to "catch up" or to fit everything into his day, easily reclaimed 20 hours a week.

With my coaching, James started his day with purpose, focused on his top priorities with specific intentions set to stay on target and get what he wanted from the day. He was now embodying the mindset of performing with time—Timefulness—being fully present in the moment, improving his quality experience and performance with time.

James reinvested his reclaimed hours by finishing the development of his online marketing course (which he successfully launched), getting back to the gym, meditating, and sleeping an extra hour every night. His success continued as he lived life without the pressure of time and free from his old, limiting beliefs. He is now living his life free from his blind spot and in charge of his time.

Now you can see that time toxins exist everywhere. As you recognize where and how toxins appear and operate, both in what you're doing and in the beliefs you hold, you will find that releasing them opens up the space for increased performance, happiness, and success.

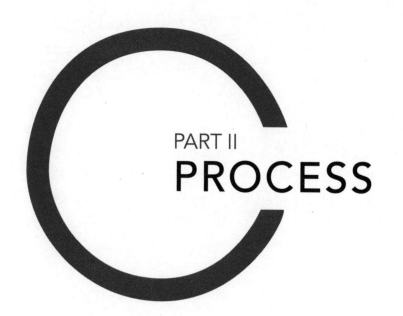

PART II
PROCESS

CHAPTER

5

The Time Cleanse

To truly cherish the things that are important to you, you
must first discard those that have outlived their purpose.
—Marie Kondō, *The Life-Changing Magic of Tidying Up:
The Japanese Art of Decluttering and Organizing*

IN THIS CHAPTER, YOU WILL BEGIN THE PROCESS
of the *Time Cleanse*. The cleanse will give you the extraordinary opportunity to really look at how you currently use your time and if you are
effectively performing with it—creating the results you want with speed,
enjoyment, and ease.

By asking the Time Cleanse question *"Is this contributing or contaminating to my happiness and success?"* in relationship to where you are spending your time, you will discover the areas where you can reclaim time and
reinvest it for what matters most in your life. This question will be your
guide going forward to take control of your time, results, and life.

As you move through the Time Cleanse, we're not striving for perfection. Instead, it's the concept of awareness followed by choice, progress, and change. The Time Cleanse will add time to your life and life to
your time while increasing your quality, experience, and performance with
time—giving you back your time for what matters most.

People, teams, and organizations find their way to me during all kinds of business and life circumstances, but often they want the following things:

- To take their business to the next level

- To have more happiness

- To learn a new skill

- To have a healthy work/life balance

- To ramp up sales or improve earnings

- To achieve rapid self-improvement

- To do a reset on themselves to get back on track

- To fully enjoy life again

- To create more great memories

- To have more free time

I've presented this tested approach to thousands of people, and one of the most remarkable results includes reclaiming a minimum of 10 hours per week—with most people getting up to 20 hours or more. The step-by-step process to *do more, get more, and be more in less time* is laid out in the coming pages. This cleanse is your foundation. Once you've had an opportunity to do the cleanse, I'll show you in Part III how to increase your results with performance techniques that you can apply to your reclaimed time.

The ultimate purpose of the Time Cleanse is for you to stop, pause, and give yourself the space and time to mindfully look at what's working for you and what's not.

Through the work you do in this chapter and the next, you will:

- *Realize* what's really important to you so you can focus on what matters most in life.

- *Recognize* where you're spending your time and where there are life toxins holding you back.

- *Release* yourself from the toxins and time contaminants hijacking your energy, time, and freedom.

- *Reclaim* your time.

- *Reinvest* it in what matters most.

The reason this close examination is so effective is that most of us are hypnotized and operating in autopilot mode that's been created by our constant busyness and distractions. We usually avoid looking at how time is spent in particular areas of our lives because we are so overwhelmed at the pace we're living at. We've been conditioned to feel that there is a limited amount of time, it's out of our control, and there's nothing we can do about it.

The Time Cleanse will shift your understanding of and relationship with time by simply acknowledging that time is not only within your influence, but something that's under your control. Let's get started.

TIME ESSENTIALS

As you go through the cleanse the first time, there are three things you need to know:

1. To start with, be open with a mindset of curiosity and discovery about how, when, where, and with whom you are spending your time. Let go of any judgments that may come up and just be with what you're discovering. When you do this, your mental and emotional state will support you in a positive way while also making this easy and fun. If you get too serious, it will slow down the process and your positive momentum. Remember: This process is about focusing on progress not perfection.

2. Be aware that you might not identify every single thing you're doing in every hour, and that's OK. You will have plenty of time

to review and add to the cleanse as you work through the book. With that being said, work through the cleanse at your own pace and take as much time as you need, but don't get stuck or overthink your answers.

3. Emotions and resistance can surface when looking at long-held patterns of *behaviors, activities, habits, people, places, or things.* This is completely normal. Just notice whatever emotions, thoughts, or feelings arise, acknowledge them, let go of any resistance to them, and continue to move through the Time Cleanse process.

The work you did in Chapter 3 when you set your goals, established your values, and connected to your why will be the foundation of this cleanse. These will act as your guides as you determine what you actually want and what you're committed to having in your life now.

Below, write in your answer to "What am I committed to having?" This will become your commitment statement. As you do this, focus on what is most important to you right now, but don't let your list extend to too many items. I suggest a maximum of three goals or one top goal that you're completely focused on. What you are writing down here is what you will be creating more time for. Remember to state your answer in the positive with as many specifics as possible. You can download the Time Cleanse Worksheet at www.timecleanse.com/book. This worksheet is one you'll refer to throughout this chapter.

Here is the format for your commitment statement:

"I am committed to having _____

(what you want) by _____ (when)."

EXAMPLE

"I am committed to and will *increase my sales by 25 percent, become more flexible with yoga, and lose 10 pounds by the end of this year.*"

Next write out your "why" for that goal that you came up with in Chapter 3.

EXAMPLE

"So I can have financial security for my family and me and be healthy to fully engage with my family."

Take the space below to fill in your commitment statement and your why:

My commitment statement:

_____

_____

My why:

_____

_____

_____

Establishing Your Commitment

> Besides the noble art of getting things done, there is the
> noble art of leaving things undone. The wisdom of life
> consists in the elimination of nonessentials.
> —Lin Yutang

Now that you've put your commitment on paper, I want you to close your eyes, take a deep breath, and imagine for a minute or two that you already have what you wrote down. Imagine you are looking through your eyes in real time as if you already have it. See what you see; hear what you hear; feel what you feel. It is now part of your life. Now notice with whom you are sharing it. How is your life different? What are you enjoying now? What does your life mean to you now that you have it? How does it feel? Take it all in. Feel it in every nerve, every fiber, and every cell of your body. Just sit with it for a moment and enjoy it all. You may even feel a smile appear as you feel it completely. Take another deep breath in, exhale, and open your eyes.

What you just experienced in that visualization serves as a breakthrough in your mind. You created a moment in time that freed you of the restrictions you place upon yourself. Now that you've seen what's possible and actually experienced what can be, I'm going to show you how to get that and do it faster than ever before.

Remember, there's only one time, and it's now. There's only one direction, and it's forward.

THE TIME CLEANSE WORKSHEET: THE EIGHT CATEGORIES OF THE TIME CLEANSE

Now that you've established what you want time for, it's time to start identifying what is supporting you and what is holding you back in the form of toxins and contaminants:

The Time Cleanse is broken down into eight main categories where toxins and contaminants can be present. You can see these in the Time Cleanse Worksheet and in the list below:

1. Technology

2. People

3. Places

4. Possessions

5. Activities

6. Professional interactions and activities

7. Thoughts and emotions

8. Out of the ordinary

I'll guide you through each category and cover them in specific detail. You may find that some of the categories overlap. The worksheet has been designed that way to make sure you identify *all* of your time. If there is an overlap, you should only account for that time in one category and just list it where it first comes up for you.

As you write out where and how much time you are spending on certain things, it's common to begin identifying what is supporting you or holding you back. But for now, let's just focus on identifying *how* you spend your time. After that, I will take you through a step-by-step process to determine how to handle those things that are contributing or contaminating to your happiness and success and what to do about it. You may find that some categories have more entries and others have less. That is normal. The key here is to identify where the majority of *your* time is currently being spent.

After we have a deeper understanding of each, you will have the space to fill in your answers for all categories on pages 94 and 95. Remember, you can download a copy of the Time Cleanse Worksheet at www.timecleanse.com/book at any time.

Before you get started, it's important to point out that you will have the opportunity to go through a detailed Business Time Cleanse, which is dedicated to specifically improving your business performance. We will do this together in Chapter 7, so don't worry if your business isn't addressed in detail in this cleanse; we will get to that later!

1. Technology

Technology offers many great things in life and can support our personal productivity, but it can also distract us from being our best. Really take a close look at technology and how you're utilizing it from day to day. How much time are you spending checking online news, Facebook, Twitter, Snapchat, Instagram, and other forms of social media, gaming, and apps?

What newsfeeds are you reading, for how long, and when? Are you playing video games? Are you on apps? Are you shopping online?

Think about these questions and estimate how much time each day you are engaged with technology. As you go through this review, let go of any judgments and don't apply any meaning to your answers. Simply get real with yourself about the amount of time you are engaged with technology each day. Write down the following:

1. Every type of engagement

2. The time of day this happens

3. For how long

With each entry, you may find it easier to write down how many hours per week you spend engaged in that activity, or it may be easier to write down how many minutes you're doing it per day. Either way is OK—whatever is easiest for you to represent your time will work.

FOR EXAMPLE:

- Spending time on Facebook (multiple times each day)
  30 minutes 5 times per week = 2.5 hours

- Going on Instagram (multiple times each day)
  1 hour 5 times per week = 5 hours

- Checking online news (7 a.m., 12 p.m., 5 p.m.)
  1 hour 7 times per week = 7 hours

2. People

Now let's consider the people you spend time with. Think about your family members, friends, acquaintances, colleagues, and coworkers. Write down the people you spend time with, both personally and professionally, and how much time you spend with them.

As you list each person, tally the number of hours or minutes you spend with that individual over a week, and note what is the usual nature of your interactions. Also be sure to include people you see less frequently and record that time as well.

Write down the following:

1. Name of the person and your relationship

2. The amount of time spent with him or her

FOR EXAMPLE:

- Bob (friend)
  3 hours per week = 3 hours

- Family
  12 hours per week = 12 hours

- Dan (coworker)
  1 hour 5 times per week = 5 hours

3. Places

Now let's think about where you spend your time. Consider your days and weekends and write down how much time you spend at home, work, the gym, restaurants, and so on. Be specific. If you go to a coffee shop for 10 minutes a day, include that, too!

Write down:

1. The place

2. What you do there

3. How long you stay

FOR EXAMPLE:

- Coffee shop (socializing)
  1 hour 5 times per week = 5 hours

- Home working
  1 hour 5 times per week = 5 hours

- Dinner at a restaurant
  2 hours 4 times per week = 8 hours

4. Possessions

What possessions do you spend your time, money, and energy on? Consider how much time you spend researching, buying, cleaning, and maintaining clothes, shoes, watches, cars, collections, and gadgets. Write down:

1. What the objects are

2. How your time is spent and how much time on each

FOR EXAMPLE:

- Researching watches
  30 minutes 5 times per week = 2.5 hours

- Car maintenance
  2 hours per week = 2 hours

- Admiring, cleaning, and organizing shoes
  3 hours per week = 3 hours

5. Activities

What activities are you engaging in? Examples include watching television, going to the movies, exercising, doing hobbies, going to a sporting event, preparing and cooking dinner, and going out for dinner or drinks with friends. Be sure to include household chores here such as cleaning and paying bills. Personal care, such as grooming, also gets included here.

As a reminder, if you've already accounted for television watching under "Technology," don't list it here a second time.

Write down:

1. What activities you are engaged in

2. How much time is spent

FOR EXAMPLE:

- Watching TV
  2 hours 5 times per week = 10 hours

- Going out for drinks
  4 hours per week = 4 hours

- Going to the gym
  1 hour 5 times per week = 5 hours

6. Professional Interactions and Activities

What are the things you do around the office on a typical workday? Do you attend meetings, organize your work, manage employees, have coworker and colleague conversations, run errands, take sales calls, or travel? And don't forget seminars, workshops, and professional trainings.

Write down:

1. The things you do while at work

2. The amount of time spent

FOR EXAMPLE:

- Meetings
  2 hours 5 times per week = 10 hours

- Sales calls
  2 hours 5 times per week = 10 hours

- Strategy conversations
  1 hour 5 times per week = 5 hours

- Work-related errands
  1 hour 3 times per week = 3 hours

7. Thoughts and Emotions

How much time do you spend on recurring thoughts, emotions, and moods? This time can include ruminating, daydreaming, projecting, fantasizing, obsessing, or worrying. How often do you experience feelings of sadness, frustration, overwhelm, or anger?

Of all the categories, this is the one where you will need to make a best guess on the amount of time you are engaged in your thoughts and emotions.

Write down:

1. Recurring thoughts and their associated feelings

2. The amount of time affected by these thoughts and feelings

FOR EXAMPLE:

- Ruminating about lost account
  30 minutes 5 times per week = 2.5 hours

- Obsessing about promotion
  1 hour 5 times per week = 5 hours

- Visualizing vacation
  10 minutes 6 times per week = 1 hour

8. Out of the Ordinary

This category is an opportunity to include anything that you've missed, is seasonal, or is out of the ordinary. You can record anything that takes your time that you've not accounted for, say, relocating, buying a house, suffering a death in the family, changing jobs, dealing with medical issues such as doctors' visits, or shopping for groceries for a sick neighbor.

Write down:

1. Anything you've missed in earlier categories, is seasonal, or is out of the ordinary

2. The amount of time that was spent

FOR EXAMPLE:

- Car shopping
  4 hours on weekends = 4 hours

- Rehabbing back injury
  1.5 hours 3 times per week = 4.5 hours

Your Time Cleanse in Action

Now that you have an understanding of each category, it's time to fill out your time and activities.

On the following pages, I have provided a blank Time Cleanse Worksheet for your entries. Later in this chapter, I'll show you how to calculate time saved, and you'll use the following worksheet throughout the chapter. As a reminder, you can download the Time Cleanse Worksheet that appears on pages 94 and 95 at www.timecleanse.com/book.

My commitment statement:

_____

_____

My why:

_____

_____

1. Technology	How much time did I reclaim per week?	___ hours

For example: checking online news, Facebook, Twitter, Snapchat, Instagram, and other forms of social media, gaming, and apps

List your own below:

_____

_____

_____

2. People	How much time did I reclaim per week?	___ hours

For example: family members, friends, acquaintances, colleagues, and coworkers

List your own below:

_____

_____

_____

3. Places	How much time did I reclaim per week?	___ hours

For example: gym, home, office, coffee shop, restaurants, the mall, and grocery store

List your own below:

_____

_____

_____

4. Possessions	How much time did I reclaim per week?	___ hours

For example: researching, buying, cleaning, and maintaining clothes, shoes, watches, cars, collections, and gadgets

List your own below:

_____

_____

_____

5. Activities	How much time did I reclaim per week?	___ hours

For example: watching television and movies, exercising, engaging in hobbies, going to a sporting event, preparing and cooking dinner, and going out for dinner or drinks with friends

List your own below:

_____

_____

_____

6. Professional interactions and activities	How much time did I reclaim per week?	___ hours

For example: attending meetings, organizing your work, managing employees, having coworker and colleague conversations, running errands, taking sales calls, or traveling

List your own below:

_____

_____

_____

7. Thoughts and emotions	How much time did I reclaim per week?	___ hours

For example: ruminating, daydreaming, projecting, fantasizing, obsessing, or worrying

List your own below:

_____

_____

_____

8. Out of the ordinary	How much time did I reclaim per week?	___ hours

For example: a death in the family, relocating, buying a house, changing jobs, dealing with medical issues such as doctors' visits, or shopping for groceries for an elderly neighbor.

List your own below:

_____

_____

_____

	Total hours reclaimed per week:	___ hours

Contributing or Contaminating?

Now that you've established where and how you spend your time, we're going to return to each answer in the eight parts of the Time Cleanse Worksheet and answer the Time Cleanse Question:

> "Is this contributing or contaminating
> to my happiness and success?"

Now it's time to go back to your worksheet and consider each item in every category. Draw a *circle* around everything you feel is *contributing* to your life (uplifting you, helping you, supporting you, moving you forward) and a *box* around every item that is *contaminating*. These items drag you down, hold you back, are unsupportive, and block you.

Be honest with yourself here. Even if something is a little toxic, put a box around it. It doesn't necessarily mean you will get rid of it, but little toxins can add up to much larger contaminations. I'll show you how to address and further evaluate those in the next few pages.

Making the Tough Choices

As you go through each category, for the majority of your entries, it may be obvious which ones are contributing or contaminating (for example: three hours of TV every night or seven hours on Facebook over the week). Others may take more consideration to determine their effect on your happiness and success. For those that are more difficult to determine, consider this example of Diane:

Diane is a good-hearted person and a longtime friend, but she tends to have only negative things to say about everything and everyone. These conversations rarely bring any contribution to your life other than producing some good feelings about your ability to be supportive and to help a friend. That aligns with your values, and you definitely don't want to ever appear selfish by not being supportive of her. Besides, you like being there for others. But the thing is, there is never any progress. It is the same thing again and again. She just wants to wallow in negativity.

If you have a "Diane"-type personality in your life, consider the following:

1. How do you feel when you are with him or her and afterward?

2. Does spending time with him or her feel like an obligation or a shared experience of mutual positive exchange?

3. Identify your interactions as one of the following:

    -   **POSITIVE/CONTRIBUTION.** Brings joy, inspiration, motivation, enthusiasm, connection, engagement, fun, spiritual aliveness, increase in your spirit; makes you feel better, more relevant. Your time spent with (fill in the blank) made a difference, felt good, energized you, created positive memories.

    -   **NEGATIVE/CONTAMINANT/TOXIN.** Leaves you drained, tired, emotional, sad, frustrated, distracted, angry, guilty, shameful, defensive, needy, addicted, out of control, suspicious, diminished, restricting. Did you feel like you were wasting your time in any way?

4. Create a simple pros and cons list to take the emotions out of it. Draw a line down the middle of a piece of paper, and on the left side, list the pros, and on the right side, list the cons. Set a timer for five minutes and write.

5. Now evaluate your answers—are they contributing or contaminating—which will give you a clear direction on what decision to make and appropriate actions to take.

This five-step exercise can be used when making difficult choices; can be applied to any *behavior, activity, habit, person, place, or thing* you face; and can provide clarity about whether something is contributing or contaminating (you can use all the questions or find one or two that will give you the clarity needed).

RECLAIMING TIME THROUGH ELIMINATING YOUR CONTAMINANTS

Now that you've looked at the areas of your life and determined what's contributing and what's contaminating, I'm going to show you how to turn the toxic hours that are contaminating you into hours that are contributing toward what you're committed to having and what matters most. In order to do this, you will be choosing one of the following options with all the contaminants you placed a box around.

1. Accept

2. Reject

3. Remove

Let's get an understanding of each option to help you make your choice.

1. Accept

Accepting is simple in concept but may take some evaluation to determine if acceptance is the appropriate choice. Here you have weighed the cost, know it's toxic, but are conscious that you are choosing not to remove it at this time.

Many factors may be at play here. When you accept this contaminant as part of your life, it means that you have considered the pros and cons of removing or changing it and determined that now may not be the right time to confront it. Perhaps it's too emotional, maybe it connects to other things that you then would have to address, or perhaps it's just too overwhelming.

No matter what the reason is, be kind to yourself and mindful in the process of acceptance.

Through this new awareness, you're now choosing to accept how things are and letting go of wanting things to be a different way (that means no whining and complaining). Letting go of these expectations allows you to release the control the contaminant has on you, but it doesn't necessarily mean the contamination is completely gone.

Every 30 days, it's a good practice to revisit each contaminant you've accepted, reevaluate it, and see what it looks like and feels like then. Awareness is an ongoing part of cleansing, and you'll gain skill as you do check-ins to see what has changed.

Just be sure you are *accepting, not tolerating*, which has an undercurrent that produces its own toxic waste in the form of growing resentment and tension. Tolerance is a coping skill that produces a tremendous psychological cost over time.

For example: You have a challenging relationship with your mother-in-law and you find the time spent with her is very toxic. She is questioning your career choice and making condescending and teasing comments to you, often in front of others, on a nonstop basis. When you leave her home after a family dinner, you don't feel good about yourself and doubt your career choices. With awareness, you decide to accept that she is who she is and acknowledge that it's nothing personal because she does it to everyone. After evaluating this dynamic, you realize it's more important to you to support your wife and ensure that your daughter gets to spend time with her grandmother.

2. Reject

When you decide to reject something in the Time Cleanse process, it may be different than you think. It means you've considered the pros and cons of changing the current relationship you have with the toxic *behavior*, *activity, habit, person, place, or thing.* It's shifting your relationship with it from its current contaminating state to one that is contributing.

There are three specific ways you can shift a contaminant to a contributor, two of which I introduced in the previous chapter, which we'll review here, plus an additional one I've added:

1. **TIME DURATION AND/OR TIME OF DAY CHANGE.** Change the amount of time you're interacting with the contaminant and/or when.

   Staying with the example from Chapter 4: You realize spending an hour a day reading or posting on Facebook is too much time on this activity. You enjoy spending time on Facebook and realize that doing it an hour a day is actually contaminating your overall happiness and success. By reducing your *time duration* to 30 minutes a day, it realigns your time in a way that's contributing to your life.

   Using the same example, you find yourself on Facebook multiple times throughout your day when you should be focused on your work activities. Changing the *time of day* when you're on Facebook to your lunch break provides better work productivity and a specific time for your uninterrupted enjoyment on Facebook.

2. **RELATIONSHIP CHANGE.** Determine what new relationship you want to have with the contaminant.

   For example: You love the relationship you have with your sister, but she continues to complain about her job, which dominates every conversation with her. You make the decision to have a conversation with her about her negativity and discuss with her how to create a new, more mutually enjoyable and supportive relationship.

Once you've identified how you will adjust your new time commitment, write it down on your worksheet. Here are two examples:

- Reading newsfeed
  1 hour 7 times per week = 7 hours
  Cut in half 30 minutes per day
    - Reclaimed time = 3.5 hours per week

- Being on Facebook
  30 minutes 7 times per week = 3.5 hours
  Cut in half 15 minutes per day
    - Reclaimed time = 1.75 hours per week

3. Remove

Removing something in the Time Cleanse is the most definitive decision. When removing, it means you've evaluated the pros and cons of the particular contaminant and determined that the cost of your time, effort, and well-being is too much to simply accept or reject—instead it must be removed entirely. As you evaluate this item, understand that removing it will allow you to get back time and energy that you can spend in more productive ways. It's also important to note that not all removals need to be permanent, and once you're back on track, you can always revisit a removal in a more balanced way if appropriate.

Let's look at removal in action.

You have been going out after work drinking socially more and more frequently. It's fun and you enjoy it, but you have an all-or-nothing personality, and you tend to stay out late. It's starting to catch up with you, as you've been missing regular sleep, have gained extra weight, and just don't feel as healthy as you want to. Even your work is beginning to suffer. You decide that the cost is too much and need to remove this from your life and regain a healthier lifestyle.

Here's an example of how to write this on your worksheet:

Going out for drinks after work
3 hours 3 times per week = 9 hours
Remove = 9 hours reclaimed per week

THE REMOVAL PROCESS TIPS

1. Internally acknowledge what you are removing. At some point, what you are removing supported, benefited, or taught you something, and it's important to recognize that. It's important to acknowledge your own growth in that you now see how this behavior, activity, habit, person, place, or thing isn't contributing to your happiness and success—and it's time to let it go.

2. It's important to take action before you talk yourself out of it or fear takes hold. Plan your action and stick to it.

Now that you understand the difference between accepting, rejecting, and removing an object, it's time to return to your worksheet to accept, reject, or remove your contaminants. Go ahead and write your changes down under each category on your worksheet on pages 94 and 95. Below is an example of how it will look.

1. Technology	How much time did I reclaim per week?	6 hours

Watching the news
- 1 hour 5 times per week = 5 hours
- Cut in half 30 minutes per day
- **Reclaimed = 2.5 hours per week**

Being on Facebook
- 1 hour 7 times per week = 7 hours
- Cut in half to 30 minutes per day
- **Reclaimed = 3.5 hours per week**

Watching Netflix
- 2 hours per week

Once you've done this for all boxed items, total your reclaimed hours for each category, and write the number of hours per week in the box for that category. Then total the collective number of reclaimed hours by adding all the numbers in the eight boxes. Enter the grand total of reclaimed hours at the bottom of the worksheet, and you'll have the exact number of hours you've reclaimed!

Here is an example of how *just* the completed reclaimed hours might look on your worksheet after you've totaled them up:

STEVEN'S SIMPLIFIED TIME CLEANSE WORKSHEET		
1. Technology	How much time did I reclaim per week?	4 hours
2. People	How much time did I reclaim per week?	4 hours
3. Places	How much time did I reclaim per week?	0 hours
4. Possessions	How much time did I reclaim per week?	0 hours
5. Activities	How much time did I reclaim per week?	6 hours
6. Professional interactions and activities	How much time did I reclaim per week?	5 hours
7. Thoughts and emotions	How much time did I reclaim per week?	2 hours
8. Out of the ordinary	How much time did I reclaim per week?	0 hours
	Total hours reclaimed per week:	21 hours

THE TIME CLEANSE IN ACTION: PAT'S STORY

My client Pat, who is in his early thirties, is a hardworking former professional athlete and successful executive in the insurance industry. When we began working together, he was very clear on the things he wanted and was ready to make them happen. He wanted to improve both his personal life and his business. In his personal life, he wanted more time with his family (wife and kids), and he also wanted to get back in better physical shape and drop the extra 15 pounds he had gained. Professionally, he wanted to grow his business and income and take his business to the next level. These were his goals for the next year.

As we began, I found that his day typically started early and ended late. His philosophy was to work harder than anyone else. That philosophy is a good one, but it was not paying the dividends he expected or wanted for the time he was putting in, and he was starting to fatigue.

He frequently would get home after 7 p.m., just crash in front of the TV, and check out . . . while his two kids and wife vied for his attention. Trying to be present with them while his gas tank was on empty wasn't working, and he knew something needed to change. That is when I took him through the Time Cleanse. He was a highly motivated guy, but until he looked at how he spent his time, none of the changes he wanted to make were going to happen. He told me when we started, "There never seems to be enough time in the day."

Pat needed a better understanding of and relationship with time. He was operating from the same place where most people start: He believed time was outside of him, was scarce, and was something he had to get good at managing. Consequently, he was fighting the clock under constant time pressure, causing tremendous fatigue and frustration. He was addicted to multitasking and trying to get it all done.

Pat shared with me that a lot of the time pressure he felt was related to his belief that he needed to get home by six for dinner and family time because he thought that's what a good husband and father should do. This was a constant cause of stress and worry.

I shared with him that he was in a values conflict, which was causing all his stress and anxiety. What we needed him to do was a values alignment. After I helped him realign his values, he realized the importance of his career and family and that he needed to be successful in his career to support his family.

His big why was being a great provider and staying fit and healthy to be there for his family over the long run.

With this new alignment, he had a discussion with his wife about their schedule and his values and commitment to her and the kids. He was amazed by how open and understanding she was when he explained his constant worry of getting home. They quickly created a schedule with their time that worked for both of them. Now when he got home, he was engaged and present and still had plenty of energy to be a great dad and husband.

As we continued to work together, I got him to see that he is the source of time and that his choices determine where he invests it. When he realized this, he was able to immediately let go of the time pressure he was always operating under. Just as importantly, he shifted to a performance mindset—Timefulness—and began to see time as an ally to help him perform at a higher level.

Next, I coached him on some performance techniques: meditation and the principles of mindfulness. I had him begin meditating at the start of his day, and in a short time, he became more focused and less reactive overall, which led him to make better choices with his time in every area of his life.

Now he was starting his day with purpose, focused on his top priorities with specific intentions set behind them. He had a clear sense of the things he wanted from the day, and he was executing them in a mindful way.

I reminded Pat that "You are the source of time and in charge of it. Time is here to serve *you*."

We then went through each category of his Time Cleanse, asking if each activity was contributing or contaminating to his happiness and success. What we found was a tremendous amount of contaminants in his business, as well as wasted time checking the news and binging on Netflix.

Pat realized he could improve his sales calls, so he became more effective and efficient talking to current and potential clients. I worked with Pat, helping him communicate with his clients in a way that set clear expectations.

Next we prioritized the right type of prospective client, so he wasn't wasting time having feel-good meetings with no business generation. He also moved many face-to-face meetings to phone calls and started cutting 45-minute meetings to 30 minutes and 30 minutes to 15 minutes.

The tool that helped him the most was a suggestion that he set a timer for every call to stay in charge of his time. That was a game changer. He reclaimed two hours a day immediately with his new time-related client meeting strategies.

Let me show you what Pat's process looked like.

PAT'S TIME CLEANSE WORKSHEET

My commitment statement:

I am committed to and will grow my business by 20 percent in sales, regain life balance with more quality time with my wife and kids, and lose 15 pounds within this year.

My why:

To be healthy and active, be a great provider for my family, and make a difference in the world with my work.

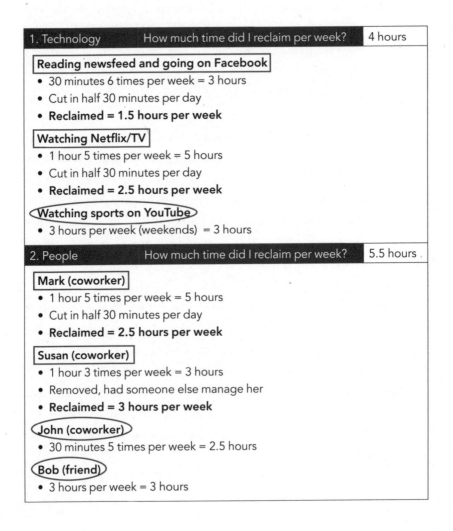

1. Technology	How much time did I reclaim per week?	4 hours

Reading newsfeed and going on Facebook
- 30 minutes 6 times per week = 3 hours
- Cut in half 30 minutes per day
- **Reclaimed = 1.5 hours per week**

Watching Netflix/TV
- 1 hour 5 times per week = 5 hours
- Cut in half 30 minutes per day
- **Reclaimed = 2.5 hours per week**

Watching sports on YouTube
- 3 hours per week (weekends) = 3 hours

2. People	How much time did I reclaim per week?	5.5 hours

Mark (coworker)
- 1 hour 5 times per week = 5 hours
- Cut in half 30 minutes per day
- **Reclaimed = 2.5 hours per week**

Susan (coworker)
- 1 hour 3 times per week = 3 hours
- Removed, had someone else manage her
- **Reclaimed = 3 hours per week**

John (coworker)
- 30 minutes 5 times per week = 2.5 hours

Bob (friend)
- 3 hours per week = 3 hours

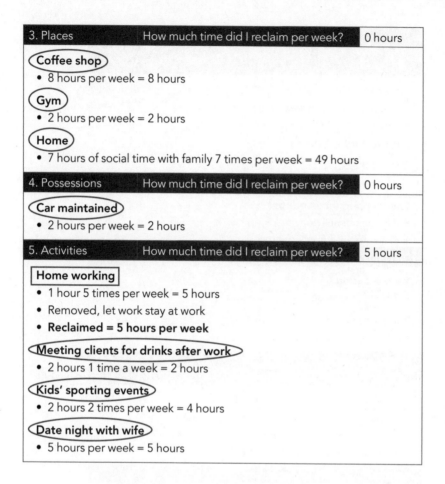

3. Places	How much time did I reclaim per week?	0 hours

Coffee shop
- 8 hours per week = 8 hours

Gym
- 2 hours per week = 2 hours

Home
- 7 hours of social time with family 7 times per week = 49 hours

4. Possessions	How much time did I reclaim per week?	0 hours

Car maintained
- 2 hours per week = 2 hours

5. Activities	How much time did I reclaim per week?	5 hours

Home working
- 1 hour 5 times per week = 5 hours
- Removed, let work stay at work
- **Reclaimed = 5 hours per week**

Meeting clients for drinks after work
- 2 hours 1 time a week = 2 hours

Kids' sporting events
- 2 hours 2 times per week = 4 hours

Date night with wife
- 5 hours per week = 5 hours

6. Professional interactions and activities	How much time did I reclaim per week?	8.5 hours

Errands
- 1 hour 2 times per week = 2 hours
- Cut in half to 1 hour a week
- **Reclaimed = 1 hour per week**

Client calls
- 3 hours 5 times per week = 15 hours

Client in-person meetings
- 3 hours 5 times per week = 15 hours
- Cut in half 1.5 hours per day
- **Reclaimed = 7.5 hours per week**

Sales meeting
- 1 hour 5 times per week = 5 hours

Paperwork
- 2 hours per week = 2 hours

7. Thoughts and emotions	How much time did I reclaim per week?	2.5 hours

Worrying about my sales numbers
- 1 hour 5 times per week = 5 hours
- Cut in half 30 minutes per day
- **Reclaimed = 2.5 hours per week**

8. Out of the ordinary	How much time did I reclaim per week?	0 hours

Home remodel
- 4 hours weekend = 4 hours

	Total hours reclaimed per week:	25.5 hours

One of the unexpected takeaways for Pat from doing the Time Cleanse was that he had always wanted his own business, but he never believed he could do it or even have the time to make it possible. As he implemented the Time Cleanse principles, he discovered new possibilities. Once Pat reclaimed his time and saw how things were changing, his big breakthrough came when he decided to open his own consulting firm. He reinvested 10-plus hours a week of his reclaimed time into his own brand and business, creating a website, logo, content, and materials—and in less than 60 days, he had opened his own consulting firm that continues to successfully grow today.

Ultimately, the cleanse gave him freedom. He never thought that sitting down with the Time Cleanse would open his eyes in a way that would lead to having his own business where he's the boss and now gets to decide whom he works with and, most importantly, gives him an abundance of time with his family while growing his income.

You can see by reviewing Pat's Time Cleanse Worksheet that the process is simple and straightforward. As you learn how to evaluate each category of the cleanse and look closely at how you are using your time, you begin to look at everything through the lens of time, helping you make better choices with using your time.

Congratulations on the completion of your first Time Cleanse. You have begun to take control of and use the great equalizer, *time*, to your benefit.

One of the best things about the Time Cleanse is that you can take it anytime and anywhere, as often as you want, continuing to improve your performance with your time.

The most important thing I can tell you is . . .

There is only one time, and it's *now*.

There is only one direction, and its *forward*.

In the next chapter, I'll show you how to build on what you've learned, and we'll start focusing on how to reinvest your reclaimed time for maximum results in the areas that matter the most to you.

6

Reinvesting Your Time

The key is in not spending time, but in investing it.
—Stephen Covey

CONGRATULATIONS! THE WORK YOU JUST DID HELPED
you to reclaim your most valuable asset—*time*!

It's time to reap the rewards of your newly reclaimed time. How, when, and with whom you reinvest your time is the key to reaching the goals you are committed to having. Just as you want to invest your money for the highest return, you want to be thinking about your time from that same investment perspective of getting the highest Return on Time, your ROT.

To establish your highest ROT, let's take a quick look at the activities in both business and life that give you your highest return on time.

Here is a list of my top ROT activities:

1. Corporate training

2. Performance research

3. Exercise at the gym

4. Planning my goals, with intentions, for the day and week

5. Speaking and keynote presentations

6. Meditating

7. Coaching my business team

8. Date night with my girlfriend

9. Connecting with friends

10. Stand-up paddleboarding

Now list your own personal activities that have the highest return on your time:

My High-Value ROT Activities

1. _____

2. _____

3. _____

4. _____

5. _____

6. _____

7. _____

8. _____

9. _____

10. _____

WHAT'S YOUR TIME WORTH?

Now that you've listed your high-ROT activities, I want you to think about what your hour is worth to you and what you can accomplish with it. Consider your day-to-day activities both at work and personally and identify where you could get back valuable time by hiring or delegating.

For me, one hour of coaching or speaking, which I'm passionate about, has much more value than an hour spent picking up my dry cleaning or running errands. So I basically "buy" back time by hiring an assistant to run errands for me.

As you go through making decisions on where to invest your reclaimed time, think about whether or not it's worth it to delegate or hire someone in order to free up an hour of your time for higher-value tasks or opportunities.

Buying Time Increases Happiness

Want more happiness? Just buy your time back. Researchers studied over 6,000 people from the United States, Canada, Denmark, and the Netherlands and found that when individuals spent money on timesaving services (housecleaning, lawn mowing, etc.), they reported having a higher level of life satisfaction—even greater than when they bought material things. They concluded that buying time can reduce time pressure and increase the quality of life.[1]

THE TIME COMPOUND EFFECT

The "compound effect" happens when you invest your time in the right things that are aligned with your why, values, and goals and contribute to your success. It then accelerates additional changes in other parts of your life. For example, one hour of exercise daily creates a higher level of fitness and energy, which can increase your productivity at work, your confidence in how you look, and the energy you have at home with your family. One hour spent with your children can make them feel more significant and, as a result, more confident in multiple areas of their lives. An extra hour of sleep can improve your business performance and overall vitality.

You see, it isn't just time; it's what you do with your time. Just one hour can have a positive compounding effect in all areas of your life.

My client Pete is the COO of a large advertising company. He had been a client of mine for several years and recently married and was now enjoying the arrival of his new daughter. He came to my office one day completely exhausted. "Steven," he proclaimed, "I have no time . . . every extra hour I have now goes to taking care of my daughter. I just don't have any time for myself."

Here is what he discovered doing the Time Cleanse. He immediately realized it had been several years since he even questioned the efficiency and productivity of his time at work. The first thing he recognized was that he was having way too many meetings, so he cut them down and got 4 hours back a week. Next he delegated some basic office responsibilities that had just become an unconscious habit and that he no longer needed to do and got 3.5 hours back per week. Lastly, he stopped hand-signing checks, which he said he had been doing for 20 years, and got 2.5 hours per week back, for a total of 10 hours a week back. That's 520 hours a year, which equals *21.6 days of his life reclaimed each year*.

Here is where the excitement came for Pete, as he told me he reinvested those reclaimed hours by taking Fridays off. He spent a half day with his daughter going to the beach and doing other fun activities, and he took the remaining hours to get in some personal reading that he enjoyed and to take extra mountain bike rides to improve his fitness.

The positive results were immediate as Pete started spending time with his daughter. He felt more connected to her and happier and more confident as a father. That improved his daily outlook tremendously. He was also getting in better shape and having more energy and mental clarity from exercising and being outdoors. These results brought huge value to the quality of his life as he reinvested his time creating better performance at work and a more balanced overall life with less stress and more fun.

ROT IN ACTION

I had been contemplating a change in my career, one in which I could make a bigger impact in the world. I mentally had made the decision, but months were going by, and the reality was that I was afraid to fully commit and actually make it happen.

A mentor of mine suggested something to help. A vision quest, he told me, was a traditional Native American spiritual journey that might help me discover what was holding me back. It is a process of solitude and reflection during which you reconnect with yourself, and that can provide insight, meaning, and direction for your life. Terrified . . . I signed up.

I was one of a small group of six arriving at the Denver airport for the vision quest. We drove 60 miles west into the mountains, up a dirt road to a log cabin sitting atop a mountain at 7,000 feet. The cabin door opened, and a woman appeared. Marilyn Young Bird, a Native American medicine woman, is a member of the Arikara and Hidatsa Nations; she's about five feet tall, with long dark hair steaked with gray. She reached her hand out to greet me and said, "I've been waiting for you." Me, not anyone else? She would be our guide for the next week, and I knew right then something special was going to happen on this mountain.

Our group started setting up tents on the mountain, where we would be sleeping. I grew up in Chicago and had never set up a tent or even camped before. As I fumbled trying to set up my one-man tent, I looked down and saw an animal paw print. As I got closer, I thought, "Oh, that's not a dog print or a deer print. That looks like a freakin' bear print!" I started freaking out thinking I'm going to die on a mountain with bears.

I immediately ran into the cabin, asking, "Marylin, are there bears here?"

She looked at me and simply said, "Yes."

She smiled and told me, "Come here." And she pointed down the narrow kitchen to the window at the end of the cabin. My heart sank when I saw two large paw prints nine feet above the ground on the outside of the window. "Yes," she said. "They are always here, always looking in."

I stumbled back, literally in shock. I said, "What do I do if a bear shows up when I'm out there?"

She said, "Oh, well, if you're standing, sit down. Then thank the bear for showing up and just pray with it."

Now at this point, I think she is absolutely crazy. She explained that the bear represents powerful medicine to Native Americans and that it is one of the highest honors if a bear shows up. I was speechless. I finished setting up my tent, but I couldn't stop thinking about the bear. My mind was now obsessed with the bear.

Two days later, with no bear sightings, the vision quest began at the sweat lodge. The sweat lodge is basically a hut, typically dome-shaped or oblong and made out of natural materials. The structure is built out of tree branches covered with blankets and sometimes animal skins. The ceremony performed within the structure may be called a purification ceremony or simply a sweat. This cleansing process prepares your mind, body, and spirit for your vision quest on the mountain.

Lava rocks are heated up in a fire next to the lodge, and they are periodically added to the center of the sweat lodge. I was sitting next to Marilyn, with the six in our group encircling the heated rocks. Marilyn started chanting. It was pitch black inside the sweat lodge, and my skin felt like it was peeling off from the heat. As she chanted, I struggled to stay in control of my mind and body as I fought the effects of the heat. It was excruciatingly hot. I kept trying to fight it. Then, finally, I couldn't take it anymore, and something took over inside of me and I just let go of the struggle. Instantly, I started feeling cooler and went into what felt like suspended time. Nearly three hours passed before we exited the sweat lodge.

I changed my clothes, grabbed my gear and tent, and made my way to the preselected place I chose on the mountain to continue my vision quest. We each had our own location in different areas of the mountain. Once I arrived, I laid out my prayer ties to form my circle. Prayer ties are created before the vision quest. They're made by placing tobacco in the center of different-colored, small cloth squares and tying each square into a little bag while placing them evenly apart and setting an intention with each one. The bags are tied together to make a long string. Traditionally, there are 405 prayer ties in total that will make up about a 10-foot-diameter circle when laid down.

I stepped into the circle, where I would remain for the next few days with no food or water. I started at about noon, and I felt pretty good. I was praying, and it started getting dark . . . and I began thinking about the bear. I started hearing the sounds of the night: the birds and the animals moving around. It became too dark to see anything. I started worrying that a bear would come and get me. I couldn't take it anymore, so I went into my tent to hide.

Now it's kind of funny, because the tent offers no protection, but the idea of shelter from the bear was psychological. I heard all kinds of animals moving around, and I went in and out of consciousness in my sleep until finally I awoke, maybe 4:30 in the morning. At daybreak, I felt it was safe to go out again, so I went back outside to continue with my meditation and prayer in the circle.

I saw the sunrise as I sat there in the dirt praying and reflecting about all the things that had happened in my life.

The focus of the vision quest is to connect with yourself and really examine your life in every aspect (inside and out). Together, the ceremonial isolation and fasting create a different state of awareness where you look at the highs and lows, turning points, successes and failures, and happy and sad times. You look at your core beliefs about yourself and the world you live in. Are they supporting you or are they against you? Do you trust or are you afraid? Who are you, and what direction is your life taking? You look at current fears and their origins. Are they really true, or can you let them go?

You look at your current relationships, those that are healthy and ones that may be toxic. You reflect on whom you're spending your time with. You review your relationship with your parents, looking at the beliefs you have adopted from them and deciding if those beliefs are valid or need to change. As you go through this process of reflection, you find forgiveness for yourself and others if needed.

You pray and meditate in whatever way works for you. You give thanks for all the events that have happened in your life, even the ones that were painful and challenging. You give thanks to your physical body, nature, and the creator. You feel grateful for all of it. Most importantly, you reflect on your life, who you are, your purpose, and what you're committed to having and creating in your life. In this process, you allow insights and wisdom to come forward in any way they may.

As the sun fully crested, I felt calm and safe. My worry of the bear was gone for now . . . I had made it through the night. The second day seemed to pass faster, but as the sun began to set, my fear began to rise even more intensely than before. I sat there praying, the sky completely black, highlighted only by the twinkling stars.

Rain started and was coming down hard, punctuated by increasing thunder and lightning. Now I had two things to worry about: the storm and the bear. When I thought things couldn't get any worse, I heard a resounding crack followed by a brilliant flash of light. A tree 50 feet from me was hit by lightning. It sounded like a stick of dynamite exploding. I couldn't take it anymore; I was at my limit. I needed to go back into my tent (womb), my safe place.

Once inside, I fell asleep, quickly and deeply. Suddenly I heard two voices going on in my head as I slept. One voice was saying, "Get up, Steven. Get out there and face your fears. Get out there and pray. You can do it." The other voice was saying, "Don't go out there. You don't need to go out there. Stay here and stay safe." These voices argued back and forth until I found myself sitting upright and awake.

That's when I had a moment of clarity. As I sat there contemplating the last couple of days on the mountain, I wondered why I was afraid of the bear; what beliefs was I making up about the bear. Marilyn wasn't afraid of the bear; why was I?

Then it hit me. When I started to reflect on my life, I could see all the places where I had created fears that weren't true. Suddenly I could see how that fear was holding me back. I could see it all very clearly now, and in that moment, I released those toxic thoughts and the emotions connected to my old, made-up beliefs. I felt an enormous sense of peace wash over me, connecting me with nature.

I stepped out of the tent and began to pray again, this time with complete clarity, no longer worried about the bear. With the fear released, I reflected more deeply on how those old fears caused me to waste so much time being distracted from connecting with my true purpose, how that had paralyzed me and kept me from taking action and moving forward. I now knew that I deeply wanted to help more people in a bigger way, helping them realize their full potential.

I began to visualize the next steps in my life and what I would be doing, what people I would be surrounded by, and what my world would look like. I created a map in my head of everything that I wanted and where I needed to start reinvesting my time, energy, and focus. I was finally ready to let go of the past and now felt confident enough to pursue my future.

I came down from the mountain the next day and reentered the sweat lodge. This time, there was no heat, and it served as a gathering place to share our visions, smoke the peace pipe, and eat natural foods. I was now ready to start living in a new way, investing my time directed by my true purpose and free from my past fears.

LESSONS LEARNED

- One moment in time can change the course of your life.
- Stopping to reflect can open your heart and mind to your true purpose.
- Fear can be the doorway to new possibilities.
- Being willing to be vulnerable allows you to connect with what matters most in your life.
- Your past doesn't have to be your future.

THE TIME IS NOW

Investing in Your Life

> Opportunities multiply as they are seized.
> —Sun Tzu, *The Art of War*

It's now time to decide where to reinvest all these newfound hours in ways that support what is truly important to you. This is what you've been working for. As a reminder, you want to use what you wrote down for "What I'm committed to having" as your guide as you go through the process of reinvesting your time.

On the worksheet there are 12 different categories to determine where you can reinvest your time.

1. Career

2. Family

3. Relationships

4. Health and fitness

5. Recreation

6. Travel

7. Personal development

8. Spiritual development

9. Hobby or new skill

10. Charity/giving back

11. Sleep/recovery/relaxation

12. Other

Start with any category that stands out to you that supports your getting what you're committed to having (from your worksheet).

- Maybe it is your family because you want to spend more time with your spouse or your kids.

- Perhaps it's your health because you want to go to the gym more and get in better shape.

- Maybe it's investing in growing your business.

- It could even be giving time to your favorite charitable cause.

Wherever you decide to reinvest your time, it's important to commit to it and write it down. As you start investing your reclaimed hours, you can always adjust your reinvested hours accordingly as you go along. The most important thing right now is to make a decision about how you are going to use your reclaimed time.

Remember Pat, the insurance professional from the previous chapter and his Time Cleanse that we went through? Let's look at his ROT worksheet so you can see how he was able to reinvest his reclaimed time.

PAT'S RETURN ON TIME WORKSHEET

My commitment statement:

I am committed and will grow my business by 20 percent in sales, regain my life balance, lose 15 pounds, and spend more quality time with my wife and kids within this year.

My why:

To be healthy and active with my family and to make a difference in the world with my work.

Total hours to reinvest per week: 25.5 hours

1. **Career**   Hours reinvested per week: 10 hours

   - Developing and setting up my own company
     3 hours per day Monday, Wednesday, Friday, and any extra free time that comes up

2. **Family**   Hours reinvested per week: 6 hours

   - Sit-down dinners with family
     1 hour 3 times per week at 6 p.m., Monday, Wednesday, Friday

   - Spend time with family and kids
     Take half day at work on Friday—3 hours

3. **Relationships**   Hours reinvested per week: 0 hours

   - No change

4. **Health and fitness**   Hours reinvested per week: 3 hours

   - Work out at my gym
     1 hour 5 times per week at 5:30 a.m., Monday–Friday

5. **Recreation**   Hours reinvested per week: 2 hours

   - Hiking
     2 hours 1 time per week
     (flexible, on a day I'm free before noon once a week)

6. Travel   Hours reinvested per week: 0 hours

   - No change

7. **Personal development**   Hours reinvested per week: 2 hours

   - Reading current business development book
     20 minutes of reading 1 hour before bed every night

8. **Spiritual development**   Hours reinvested per week: 1.5 hours

   - Meditation
     20 minutes a day 5 a.m. every day

9. **Hobby or new skill**   Hours reinvested per week: 0 hours

   - No change

10. **Charity/giving back**   Hours reinvested per week: 1 hour

    - Consulting for local nonprofit
      1 hour Saturday mornings before noon

11. **Sleep/recovery/relaxation**   Hours reinvested per week: 0 hours

    - No change

12. **Other**   Hours reinvested per week: 0 hours

    - No change

I, _____, am committed to my calendar
and to follow through with all my ROT hours to the best of my ability.

Sign/date_____

Now it's your turn to reinvest your time.

Be specific and begin committing to a specific day, place, and time (with whom, what, when, where, and how). For example, commit to an hour at the gym on Monday, Wednesday, and Friday at noon; set aside two hours a week volunteering for your favorite charity on Saturday; spend an hour each Thursday morning practicing your hobby. As you write each one down, think about the intentions behind each commitment and your why behind it.

Write your commitments down on your ROT Worksheet provided on page 125 in this chapter. Once that's done, it's important to make sure you *enter them in your calendar* as a way to reinforce your resolve. By doing this, you can keep track of your time and at any point ask yourself, "Am I following up with my commitments?" This is your guide going forward, so make sure that you're investing time in the right places.

Note that at the end of the ROT Worksheet, there is a place for your signature. I want you to sign it to memorialize your commitment, which will help hold you accountable to following through with your time and what you're committed to having. You can download this worksheet at www.timecleanse.com/book.

Once you sign this agreement, a great technique to support your progress that I learned from David Goggins, the author of *Can't Hurt Me*, is the Accountability Mirror.[2] Applying his technique and using your ROT Worksheet as a guide, ask yourself while looking into a mirror, "Did I follow through with my time commitments to improve myself?"

Goggin suggests being brutally honest with yourself and then making any adjustments needed for the following day.

A quote I love of David's is "One day you can take off, not today." So, follow your time commitments!

MY RETURN ON TIME WORKSHEET

My commitment statement:

My why:

Total hours to reinvest per week: _____

1. **Career**   Hours reinvested per week _____

2. **Family**   Hours reinvested per week _____

3. **Relationships**   Hours reinvested per week _____

4. **Health and fitness**   Hours reinvested per week _____

5. **Recreation**   Hours reinvested per week _____

6. **Travel**   Hours reinvested per week _____

7. **Personal development**   Hours reinvested per week _____

8. **Spiritual development**   Hours reinvested per week _____

9. **Hobby or new skill**   Hours reinvested per week _____

10. **Charity/giving back**   Hours reinvested per week _____

11. **Sleep/recovery/relaxation**   Hours reinvested per week _____

12. **Other**   Hours reinvested per week _____

I, _____, am committed to my calendar
and to follow through with all my ROT hours to the best of my ability.

Sign/date_____

By reinvesting your time, you have now reclaimed your most valuable asset, *time*, for what you're most committed to having. Now that you have mastered the Time Cleanse process, we will turn our attention to your business and/or career to have the same great results in an area that I know is of big importance to you.

CHAPTER

7

The Time Cleanse for Business Performance

You've only got three choices in life:
Give up, give in, or give it all you've got.
—U.S. Navy SEALs

NOW THAT YOU'VE HAD SOME EXPERIENCE WITH the Time Cleanse, let's turn our view specifically to business. In this chapter we'll use the Time Cleanse to achieve the goals that drive our careers forward, provide the income for our dreams, and give us the confidence we need to make a difference.

Going forward, the terms "career" and "business" will be interchangeable. The answers you give in your Business Time Cleanse will include both your broader career and the way you make a living, which can be working for a company, working for yourself as a solopreneur, or being an entrepreneur who owns a company and has employees.

Much like the Time Cleanse, the Business Time Cleanse revolves around the question "What are you committed to having?" but with a focus on business, whether that be a career or a company you have started.

The Business Time Cleanse is a process that will bring tremendous value, even the first time you engage in it, but I highly recommend that you continue to do it every month, quarter, and year. It is a powerful process that will serve as your guide. Investing in it periodically will drive continual business improvement.

BEFORE WE GET STARTED

Key Questions to Ask Yourself About You and Your Business or Career

Before we dive into the Business Time Cleanse, take a few minutes to reflect on and write out a few answers to each of the following questions related to your business/career. This exercise will open your thought process and prime your mind for the Business Time Cleanse.

- What am I doing in my business or career? Why?

  _____

  _____

  _____

- How am I doing it? Why?

  _____

  _____

  _____

- With whom am I doing it? Why?

  _____

  _____

  _____

- Who or what is distracting me or holding me back?

  _____

  _____

  _____

- What activities do I absolutely *not* want to be doing in my business/career?

  1. _____

  2. _____

  3. _____

  4. _____

  5. _____

  6. _____

  7. _____

- What activities bring my greatest Return on Time (ROT) and business growth?

  1. _____

  2. _____

  3. _____

  4. _____

  5. _____

  6. _____

  7. _____

Evaluate Your Business

As you begin the Business Time Cleanse, it's helpful to get a clear understanding of how the different aspects of your business are performing. By evaluating each area, you will increase your awareness of where your potential performance gaps are.

To begin, rate each of the following categories with you and your business in mind using a scale of 1 to 10 (10 being the highest satisfaction level and 1 being the lowest). This quick evaluation helps you see areas where you are doing well and areas that need improvement.

QUICK EVALUATION										
Sales	1	2	3	4	5	6	7	8	9	10
Management	1	2	3	4	5	6	7	8	9	10
Leadership	1	2	3	4	5	6	7	8	9	10
Operations	1	2	3	4	5	6	7	8	9	10
Business growth	1	2	3	4	5	6	7	8	9	10
Product development	1	2	3	4	5	6	7	8	9	10
Marketing/promotion	1	2	3	4	5	6	7	8	9	10
Personal performance	1	2	3	4	5	6	7	8	9	10
Customer service	1	2	3	4	5	6	7	8	9	10
Human resources	1	2	3	4	5	6	7	8	9	10

Now that you are aware of where you can and would like to improve, it's time to begin the Business Time Cleanse!

BUSINESS TIME CLEANSE WORKSHEET

In the following section, I will be taking you step by step through the Business Time Cleanse Worksheet, which can be found on page 137 and downloaded at www.timecleanse.com/book.

Just as I did in the Time Cleanse in Chapter 5, I have included an example from one of my clients, who successfully completed the Business Time Cleanse. At any point, feel free to reference his cleanse at the end of this chapter to help you in your process.

Step 1. Establish What You Are Committed to Having Now in Your Business or Career

The most important part of the Business Time Cleanse is to start by laying the groundwork for the rest of the process by identifying what you are committed to having right now in your business or career. Take some time to think about what you need to do to take your business to the next level. List up to three top goals you are focused on achieving to make that happen.

When determining your goals, you can identify them as one-year, quarterly, or monthly goals. Just be sure the goals are appropriate to you right now.

Here are some examples to inspire you before you get started:

- "I will increase my business production 30 percent this year."

- "I will reduce operating costs by 15 percent within the next six months."

- "I will change my workweek from five days to four by the end of the quarter."

Now it's your turn. Write your goals down here to get started; those will be the goals you're committed to having in your business or career.

What am I committed to having now in my business or career?

1. _____

2. _____

3. _____

Next, as you've done previously in the Time Cleanse, fill in below your "why" for the goals you're committed to having in your business or career.

My why:

_____

_____

Step 2. Understand How You Are Spending Your Time

To understand how you are spending your time, write down every single business activity you engage in (include the time of day and the frequency, when appropriate) on page 137.

Next, just as you did with the Time Cleanse, ask the Time Cleanse Question: "Is this contributing or contaminating to my happiness and success?" Then put a *circle* around what *contributes* and a *box* around what *contaminates*. Here is an example.

Step 3. Ask Yourself the Following Questions

Now that you've determined whether a specific task is contributing or contaminating to your time, you have to decide whether or not you should keep doing it and how. While this may sound similar to the "accept, reject or remove" portion of the Time Cleanse, the Business Time Cleanse is different in that we'll instead ask specific business performance questions that require a yes-or-no answer *only*.

Let's get started with each of the questions. As you move through the worksheet, you will see the Notes column on the far right side. It's important to fill this out with appropriate notes as you go along to guide you in the action steps for each activity.

Question 1. "Should I keep doing this?"

ACTIVITY	KEEP DOING THIS? (YES/NO)	IMPROVE THIS? (YES/NO)	DELAY DOING THIS? (YES/NO)	DELEGATE/ AUTOMATE/ OUTSOURCE THIS? (YES/NO)	HOURS RECLAIMED PER WEEK	NOTES

With the activity listed, ask yourself should this activity still be done? (Choose yes or no.)

Question 2. "Can I improve this?"

ACTIVITY	KEEP DOING THIS? (YES/NO)	IMPROVE THIS? (YES/NO)	DELAY DOING THIS? (YES/NO)	DELEGATE/ AUTOMATE/ OUTSOURCE THIS? (YES/NO)	HOURS RECLAIMED PER WEEK	NOTES

With the activity listed, can you improve how it's being done? (Choose yes or no.) If yes, ask yourself how? Here are some areas to consider for how you could improve it:

- The time of day

- Duration or frequency of activity

- Is there a different strategy for doing it?

- Should someone else do it?

Make appropriate notes in the last column for any changes.

Question 3. "Should I delay doing this?"

ACTIVITY	KEEP DOING THIS? (YES/NO)	IMPROVE THIS? (YES/NO)	DELAY DOING THIS? (YES/NO)	DELEGATE/ AUTOMATE/ OUTSOURCE THIS? (YES/NO)	HOURS RECLAIMED PER WEEK	NOTES

With the activity listed, should I delay doing it? (Choose yes or no.)

If yes, delay until when and for how long? (Enter your answer in the Notes column.)

Question 4. "Should I delegate/automate/outsource this?

ACTIVITY	KEEP DOING THIS? (YES/NO)	IMPROVE THIS? (YES/NO)	DELAY DOING THIS? (YES/NO)	DELEGATE/ AUTOMATE/ OUTSOURCE THIS? (YES/NO)	HOURS RECLAIMED PER WEEK	NOTES

With the activity listed, should I delegate/automate/outsource this? (Choose yes or no.)

If yes, ask what is the best option to delegate/automate/outsource? (Enter your answers in the Notes column.)

Now it's time for you to fill out your Business Time Cleanse Worksheet. You'll find it on page 137. I have provided you an example Business Cleanse completed on page 138 to help guide you in this process. Remember, you can also download the Business Time Cleanse Worksheet at www.timecleanse.com/book.

BUSINESS TIME CLEANSE WORKSHEET						
ACTIVITY	KEEP DOING THIS? (YES/NO)	IMPROVE THIS? (YES/NO)	DELAY DOING THIS? (YES/NO)	DELEGATE/ AUTOMATE/ OUTSOURCE THIS? (YES/NO)	HOURS RECLAIMED PER WEEK	NOTES
Total hours reclaimed per week: _____						

BUSINESS TIME CLEANSE WORKSHEET SAMPLE

ACTIVITY	KEEP DOING THIS? (YES/NO)	IMPROVE THIS? (YES/NO)	DELAY DOING THIS? (YES/NO)	DELEGATE/ AUTOMATE/ OUTSOURCE THIS? (YES/NO)	HOURS RECLAIMED PER WEEK	NOTES
Sales calls • 10 hours; 2 hours a day before 10 a.m.	Yes	Yes	No	No		Cluster sales calls into 1-hour time blocks before noon
Customer follow up • 2 hours per week	No	Yes	N/A	Yes, delegate	2	Train my assistant how to do follow up customer calls
Talk with coworker • 10 hours per week	Yes	Yes	No	No	4	Limit my conversation time with Justin, as he has a tendency to create drama
Go for coffee • 4 hours per week	Yes	Yes	No	No	3	Limit time socializing to 15 minutes
Organize office and documents • 5 hours per week	No	Yes	Yes	Yes, delegate	5	Have my assistant organize office documents at the end of each day
Check Facebook • 30 minutes per day	Yes	Yes	No	No	3	Stop checking Facebook for social reasons
Check online news • 30 minutes per day	Yes	Yes	Yes, delay	No	2	Limit checking news to 1 time a day at lunchtime for 10 minutes
Generate monthly reports • 3 hours per week	No	Yes	No	Yes, automate	3	Implement automated sales software for monthly reports
Total hours reclaimed per week:					22	

Step 4. Determine How Much Time You Reclaimed from Each Activity

Now that you have completed filling out the Business Cleanse, use the worksheet to calculate the total number of hours you reclaimed for each category per week and enter that number in the space provided for each category.

Step 5. Discover How Much Total Time You Just Got Back for Yourself

Now add up the hours reclaimed from each category for a grand total and fill that in at the bottom of the worksheet in the "Total hours reclaimed per week" box.

Reviewing Your Completed Worksheet

Make sure you've written clear notes on the action steps for each item. You'll be utilizing those notes and action steps when you reinvest your time in the following Return on Time (ROT) Business Worksheet.

RETURN ON TIME BUSINESS WORKSHEET

Reflecting on what you wrote on your worksheet for "What am I committed to having now in my business or career?" write out where you are reinvesting your time. Get specific. Write in who, what, when, how, the day, time of day, frequency, and amount of time needed to achieve your goals. Then write in specific action steps to implement. Once this is completed, it is vital that you calendar each activity with the appropriate amount of time blocked out for it.

Follow these steps to fill out the ROT Business Worksheet on page 141 or download at www.thetimecleanse.com/book:

1. In the "Activity" column, write what activity you will be doing.

2. In the "Hours Reinvesting Per Day or Week" column, write how much time you will reinvest.

3. Then fill in what action steps you'll take in the "Actions" column.

4. Lastly, write any notes that will help guide and support you in taking action.

Here is a brief example.

ACTIVITY	HOURS REINVESTING PER DAY OR WEEK	ACTIONS	NOTES
Sales calls	1 hour per day	Cluster sales calls into 1-hour time block before noon	Nonnegotiable; this is the key to my business growth
Research market trends	3 hours per week	Do online research for market trends between 3 and 4 p.m.	This activity can be implemented in any of my free downtime
Client lunches for networking	4 hours per week	Schedule and take out key clients to discuss further product engagement	Communicate with my assistant to schedule lunches

RETURN ON TIME WORKSHEET			
ACTIVITY	HOURS REINVESTING PER DAY OR WEEK	ACTIONS	NOTES

THE BUSINESS TIME CLEANSE IN ACTION: CHARLES' STORY

My client, Charles, is a luxury real estate broker in Los Angeles. He had some serious health problems that put his business success in jeopardy. He was into the third quarter of his year and was way behind in sales and income. He only had a few short months to turn things around and get back on track. With over half the year already gone, that seemed impossible to Charles, especially since he still wasn't 100 percent healthwise. He felt defeated and overwhelmed.

As we sat together, I explained to him that it was possible to "compress time" in the sales cycle if he was willing to commit to the Business Time Cleanse process. In his desperation, he agreed.

As I began my coaching, the first step was to challenge and shift his belief about how long a sale takes to complete. We all have a preconceived belief about how long a sale takes (which is usually not 100 percent true).

I asked Charles, "Is it possible for you to perform a year's worth of sales in ten months?" He thought for a moment and said yes. Then I asked if it was possible in nine months, in six months . . . even in four months. Although uncomfortable, Charles continued to nod his head yes. It would be extremely hard work, but it was technically possible if everything went perfectly.

Finally, I got Charles down to two months—could he perform a year's worth of record sales in eight weeks' time? He knew it was possible, but he didn't think he could do it, which is normal for most people when they first hear this. That was all about to change.

Now that we established it was possible, we got to work on implementing the Business Time Cleanse and took a hard look at what was contributing to hitting his sales goals and what was contaminating his efforts.

What I do with business clients when it comes to sales goals and growing their business is to find out what top activities are needed to generate sales. I asked Charles, "What is the number one activity you need to do to hit your goal?"

Without hesitation, he said, "10 by 10. I need to make 10 sales contacts by 10 a.m. as a minimum daily."

"Great," I said, "I'm going to help you create the environment to make that happen."

He needed to sell 10 homes in 8 weeks, and that's what he set his goal for and committed to.

Then I asked him the why question: "Why is it important to hit this sales goal?" He said he wanted to continue his lifestyle once he retired and be able to give back through his philanthropy efforts. The more money he made, the more he could help people.

I had Charles first list all the activities of his business day and personal life to determine what was contributing or contaminating. After he saw what was contaminating him and his business, I had him make a list of things he would no longer be doing in the future—hooks, triggers, and time-wasters—what I call a "never-to-do list." They included:

- Watching more than one hour of Netflix a day

- Having sports conversations with staff

- Engaging in any conversation without a preset time limit

- Running errands during the day

- Randomly browsing online

Next, I took him through the Business Time Cleanse, as you can see on the following two pages.

CHARLES' BUSINESS TIME CLEANSE WORKSHEET

ACTIVITY	KEEP DOING THIS? (YES/NO)	IMPROVE THIS? (YES/NO)	DELAY DOING THIS? (YES/NO)	DELEGATE/ AUTOMATE/ OUTSOURCE THIS? (YES/NO)	HOURS RECLAIMED PER WEEK	NOTES
Going to the coffee shop • 8 hours	Yes	Yes	No	No	5	Set timer on phone when taking a break at the coffee shop; limit to 20 minutes per visit
Sales calls • 10 hours	Yes	Yes	No	No		Make calls before 10 a.m. and increase call time blocking to 1 hour
Follow up on current deals • 5 hours	Yes	Yes	No	Yes, delegate	2.5	Have my assistant do the majority of follow ups
Nonrevenue client conversions • 8 hours	Yes	Yes	No	No	4	Reduce time engaged in nonclient conversations
Daily team meetings • 5 hours	Yes	Yes	No	No	2.5	Change schedule to 15-minute a.m. meeting and 15-minute p.m. meeting

Task						
Assistant meetings • 4 hours	Yes	Yes	No	No	2	Reduce meetings to 20 minutes a.m. and 20 minutes p.m.
Listing presentations • 6–10 hours	Yes	No	No	No		
Weekly corporate meeting • 3 hours	Yes	Yes	Yes	No	3	Temporarily stop for 2 months
Client lunches/dinners • 8 hours	Yes	No	No	No		Continue scheduling lunches and dinners
MLS researching for buyer or clients • 5 hours	Yes	Yes	No	Yes, delegate	3	Give instructions to my assistant and have him do research
Marketing and social media • 5 hours	Yes	Yes	No	Yes, outsource	5	Hire social media firm to handle all social media activities
Total hours reclaimed per week:					27 hours	

After going through the Business Time Cleanse, Charles was amazed when he reclaimed 27 hours for himself and his business. He told me he had no idea there was that much he could get back.

We then strategized where he could best reinvest his reclaimed time to reach his sales goals. His Return on Time Worksheet looked like this:

CHARLES' RETURN ON TIME WORKSHEET			
ACTIVITY	HOURS REINVESTING PER DAY OR WEEK	ACTIONS	NOTES
Sales calls	8 hours per week	Cluster sales calls into 2 one-hour time blocks before noon to do all at once	Nonnegotiable; this is the key to my business growth
Research market trends	3 hours per week	Do online research for market trends between 3 and 4 p.m. Find pocket listings	This activity can be implemented in any of my free downtime
Client lunches/ dinner/events for networking	4 hours per week	Schedule and take out key clients to discuss further product engagement	Communicate with my assistant to schedule lunches
Exercise	5 hours per week	Schedule exercise 7 a.m. 5 times per week at the gym	This is nonnegotiable; this is important for reducing stress and staying fit so I can perform at my best; 5 workouts per week
Review weekly goals/set daily intentions/ meditate	2.5 hours per week	Prework routine to review goals, set my daily intention, and do my 10-minute meditation	This is key to getting my day started right
Drive my real estate sales area prospecting	3 hours per week	Drive my neighborhood for potential homes to make blind offers on	This can add 2 to 5 extra sales a year from my past history of doing it
Office meeting	1.5 hours per week	Have my assistant schedule lunch meeting	This is important for our growth as a company, to promote a deeper connection, motivation, and common purpose as a team

Once I took Charles through the Business Time Cleanse process and he understood where and how he needed to reinvest his time, the transformation began.

I immediately implemented some performance tools to accelerate his results. Each morning, I had him start with a meditation session before he got into the office. This helped him get centered and ready for the day. He quickly found that his morning meditation helped him be more focused, mindful, and energized. He felt more in control and less reactive and was able to more consciously respond to the day as it came at him.

In addition to his a.m. meditation, I had him establish his three top priorities for his day with specific intentions behind them to help ensure he was absolutely focused on them during the day.

He completely took on the belief that he was the source of time and in charge of it, letting go of the old belief that it was something outside of him and not in his control.

I coached him to calendar every single thing he had planned for the day, blocking out the appropriate time for each commitment. He hit his 10 calls before 10 a.m. every day!

Each evening, he reviewed his day and prepared for the next. He also took my suggestions on a sleep routine and began to get regular nights of quality sleep, which he hadn't had in months.

His energy and focus shifted to the right revenue-generating activities, and once he got going on the plan, I could see the sparkle in his eye when the deals started quickly closing one after another. I watched the compounding effect take over. He completely took on the mindset of Timefulness—he was now performing with time.

He said, "Once I kept my focus on where I put my time by calendaring everything and started to recover more effectively every day by getting more sleep, I felt the momentum shift and the results started compounding. I now realized how valuable and important my time is and where to invest it. I have to protect my time and attention from being hijacked, and when I do that, I'm unstoppable."

After his eighth week, Charles hit is goal: He closed 10 deals—the most deals and revenue he had ever done in such a short amount of time. The momentum continued for the rest of the year, helping him hit his all-time sales record over his 25-plus year career.

Now that you have mastered the Business Time Cleanse, it's time to turn our attention to how to increase your results. In the next section of the book, dedicated to performance, you will learn how to maximize every hour with tools, tactics, and tips to perform at your highest level, as well as with teams, colleagues, and coworkers.

PART III
PERFORM

CHAPTER

8

Performance
with People

Knowing others is wisdom,
knowing yourself is enlightenment.
—Lao Tzu

ONE MY FAVORITE SAYINGS IS, "YOU ALWAYS DO IT
yourself, but you never do it alone," because the fact is that there are always
people who help us and whom we need to work with. It is our ability to
communicate, connect, and collaborate with others that brings out our full
potential, as well as theirs.

In this chapter, I will explain the different Time Types so you can
determine which you are and learn how to work with others more effectively. I will also show you how to start saying no to the things that are
stealing your time and how to effectively communicate with others in a
way that maximizes your time and overall time performance.

THE TWO TIME TYPES

Now that you have mastered the Time Cleanse process, I will explain
the different Time Types so you understand how you might work best
with your new time—and work with others who are like and unlike you.

By understanding Time Types and how they impact you, you will create stronger relationships, as well as increase your performance with others and teams.

As we mature from early childhood to adulthood, we begin to learn about time and how it works. In the beginning, we had no responsibility for time; our caretakers were responsible for our every moment. As we progressed, we learned how to tell time on our own and came to understand that the world ran by the measurement of it. This likely started when we first went to school because we needed to arrive at a certain time and hand in assignments on specific dates, etc. Influenced by these requirements, we began to place value on things like schedules, punctuality, and deadlines.

Eventually, this resulted in our measuring life by units of time, which then extended to others, and we began valuing others based on their relationship with time in comparison with our relationship with it. Today, we project our own rules onto others and have beliefs around how others value us based on their relationship with time.

Through my teaching and coaching, I have come to understand that there are two Time Types, which I have defined as the Time Watchdog and the Time Lounger. Over time, each of us has developed to be one of the two.

The Time Watchdog

The Watchdog has an intense adherence to anything time related: structure, organization, precision, and rules. Clocks, alarms, and measures are set to cue you when things are supposed to happen. You follow a schedule and a system that brings order and predictability. You have high value and respect for punctuality and being on time. The Time Watchdog can add pressure to self and others through inflexibility and judgment when there is variance or when others don't adhere to the Watchdog's strict standards around time.

The Time Lounger

If you are a Lounger, you believe that time will bend to your will. You feel at ease with time, but to others, you may appear chaotic or flighty. You believe things will happen when they are supposed to and that time unfolds rather than operates in a carefully measured manner. You frequently get lost in the present moment, which likely affects others more than you. But Time Loungers can also become defensive by overexplaining why they're late, which can give the appearance of being irresponsible, not caring, or feeling misunderstood.

DETERMINE YOUR TIME TYPE

Read through the lists below and put a check mark next to the statements that apply to you:

Watchdog

❑   I am structured and disciplined in my daily tasks.

❑   I am usually early or on time to meetings, appointments, and social engagements.

❑   I feel frustrated, angry, or disrespected when someone shows up late.

❑   I think lateness is a character flaw.

❑   I calculate how much time something will take before doing it.

❑   I often monitor how others deal with time and police them if needed.

❑   I take pride in the fact that I am always on time.

Lounger

❏   I am usually barely on time, a little late, or a lot late to meetings, appointments, and social engagements.

❏   Even though I could be late, I still grab a coffee while "on my way."

❏   I often think I can do one more thing before an appointment.

❏   It's easy for me to get lost in things I enjoy and lose track of time.

❏   I tend to value what is happening in the moment more than what will happen in the future.

❏   The freedom of an open schedule calms or invigorates me.

❏   Losing track of time helps me feel creative and present in the moment.

Take a second to notice where you've placed your check marks.

If more of your check marks are under "Watchdog," you are structured and disciplined with time. You consider time a valuable asset that you respect for yourself and others. You pride yourself on being on time and even arrive or deliver early, which makes you feel great. You can have difficulty with people who show up late and don't have the same view of time as you do. You often remind people about time and hold them accountable for being late. You want them to take some responsibility!

If you are a Lounger, you appreciate the freedom of life without restriction. Showing up on time is not your priority. You like the flexibility of doing things on your time and often lose track of time. It isn't that you don't respect time; instead you aren't willing to get stressed out over being a little late, and you value the present moment more than the future. You also can get frustrated and irritated when people make a big deal about your being late.

Knowing these Time Types and the characteristics of each allows you to see the difference in others and have more empathy, compassion, and understanding for their style.

A few other things to remember when it comes to Time Types are:

1. Don't take other people's Time Types personally.

2. Time Types aren't absolute. You can have a different Time Type in various areas of your life, as well as in varying degrees. Perhaps you are a Time Lounger in your personal life and a Time Watchdog at work.

3. When life happens, your Time Type may be challenged. Watchdogs are usually prepared, while Time Loungers likely won't to be able to keep up with change in the same way. Stay flexible and know there will be different responses.

TIME TYPES IN ACTION

It's no secret that the fundamental success of business is based on time and how it's used. Performance results require adherence to schedules, deadlines, appointments, and meetings. Your Time Type could have a profound impact on the way people view you, your ability to advance in your career, your effectiveness on teams, and the perception of your overall performance.

If you are a Lounger and don't meet deadlines or are consistently late to meetings, etc., it could have a detrimental effect on team cohesion, job performance, your career, and people's perceptions of you.

On the flip side, if you are a Watchdog and overreact, hold strict standards, lack empathy, and are inflexible, this can equally impact your relationships and effectiveness with others.

The key here is to have an open dialogue and create agreed-upon guidelines on time-related issues. This eliminates potential stress and pressure between different Time Types on the team, which creates an environment that flourishes. Everyone will know what's expected and have pre-agreements in place about how to adjust if there is any variance to the schedule.

Time Types and Meetings

Starting a meeting late affects everyone involved. We've all been irritated at one time or another by the person who holds up the group.

By having a strategy in place (for example, asking latecomers to join in quietly and ask any questions about information they may have missed if they need context or relevance), the expectation of how lateness will be managed will be clear from the start. If you think about one person being 10 minutes late when attending a meeting with five other participants, you may realize this person collectively used or wasted 50 minutes of time! This way of thinking can help improve our accountability for our own time and that of others.

Time Types in Relationships

I was in a new relationship with promise. We had been dating for just a month or two and enjoyed many of the same things. Everything was going great, and we were increasingly enjoying each other's company. Then something started to happen that took me off guard. She was starting to be late.

At first it was a few minutes here and there. It bothered me, but I didn't want to make a big deal about it. Then it began to happen more frequently. What was once 5 minutes late from time to time was now regularly 20 minutes late. So I decided we needed to have a talk about it. We sat down, and I asked why she couldn't show up on time or be ready on time when I picked her up.

She immediately became defensive, telling me it wasn't her fault and giving one reason after another. She explained that she plans to be on time and things just happen. She also couldn't understand why I was making such a big deal out of it. After all, it was just a few minutes. All her explanations seemed to me at the time complete nonsense. She is a smart woman with a professional career that requires her to be at work on time. Why couldn't she be on time for me?

Well, the talk only made things worse; more fights about time. Now I was looking at my watch, predicting her being late, and wanting her to be late so I could be right . . . crazy, right? The more often she was late, the more I watched the clock, and the pressure was about to explode between us.

As time went on, I could see that I was letting my frustration get the best of me and was not communicating in a positive way. And it was negatively affecting a relationship that I valued. Like many of us, she and I had attached so much meaning to each other's behavior, all while holding ourselves up as having good reasons for behaving the way we each did.

I eventually came to this resolution: She genuinely wants to be on time, and she doesn't want to disrespect me and our time together; she just has a different time style than I do. She likes the freedom from a schedule and not having to stress over being someplace at a certain time. She loves getting lost in the present moment and enjoying whatever she may be doing, which makes her feel creative and alive, and by doing so, she frequently loses track of time.

Through conversation, we realized that she has the ability to get anywhere she wants on time. She is always punctual to work, flights, doctor's appointments, etc. It's stressful to her to be on a regimented schedule during her downtime. Besides, most of the people in her personal life just accept that's how she is.

Through those same conversations, we discovered, on the other hand, that I had a very different relationship with time. Being on time is really important to me and is something I focus on daily. I feel stressed if I'm late and not on schedule and believed from my childhood upbringing that if people were late, they were being disrespectful of me and my time. This belief set me up for many disappointments and for my personalizing things that had nothing to do with me. It was clear from talking with her that she never intended to disrespect me and genuinely wanted to be on time and enjoyed our time together as much as I did.

This conversation brought to light some major insights that put our relationship back on course. (1) People have different relationships with time based on their personality and upbringing, which now I call Watchdog and Lounger. (2) Neither style is better or worse; they are just different. (3) Differences can complement each other.

When we sat down and talked it out, we recognized our differences and could understand each other more completely. After all, we loved the unique differences we both brought to the relationship beyond our Time Types that attracted us to each other. Now we both had more compassion and understanding of our styles. We created agreements around our time together that were a good compromise with both of our styles and supported our relationship to connect deeper with more meaning and love.

While this story is one focused on dating, it relates to every relationship we have both in business and in our personal lives. Among the many individuals and organizations I've worked with, I've personally seen the cost of Time Types clashing with each other. You most likely have already begun to reflect on different situations and people in your life with similar and different Time Types. Perhaps it's a colleague or client who drives you crazy because he or she is always late. Or it's a coworker who overreacts when someone is late to a meeting and is hostile toward the person for the entire meeting. When I teach that Time Types have distinctive characteristics, I can see the smiles of relief of workshop participants and clients who finally understand that it wasn't personal; it was just a clash of Time Types.

By understanding the characteristics of these Time Types and how they developed, you no longer need to take any differences personally; it's just their Time Type. This can allow meaningful conversations to take place and result in agreements around time that create a positive working relationship.

TIME TYPE REFLECTIONS

Now that you know your Time Type, let's consider how it may be impacting others at work and in life. Ask yourself the following questions and write down your answers to them:

1. How does my Time Type support me and my colleagues, clients, and friends?

    _____

    _____

2. How is my Time Type affecting others in a positive or negative way?

    _____

    _____

3. What adjustments, if any, could I make to increase my connection, engagement, and performance with them?

    _____

    _____

TIME TYPE STRATEGIES

Now that you've seen the different Time Types in action, the following strategies I've developed will help you perform more effectively with others and in teams.

1. **Identify your Time Type and have some fun sharing the information with others you interact with.** Whether it's in your personal relationships in life or your professional relationships at work, knowing the Time Type of the people around you is helpful. Don't assume their Time Type for them, but instead help them under-

stand for themselves. Knowing the style of another has the potential to save time and improve performance for both of you.

2. **Have a discussion about Time Types personally and professionally to understand your unique style and preferences about time.** This will eliminate the stories we make up about people's actions around their relationship with time and allow a deeper understanding of how to navigate for best results with the people in your life.

3. **Make healthy agreements about how to work and play that honor everyone's style, so they can perform at their best.** Creating agreements around time establishes an atmosphere of trust, safety, and respect while honoring the unique styles we each have.

4. **Create a predetermined strategy to deal with any upsets that may arise.** There is a saying in couples counseling: "One of the most important skills for long-lasting, successful relationships is the ability to repair upsets quickly and in an empathetic way." Have a strategy to talk things out when upsets occur.

With all these strategies, have some fun celebrating your Time Type differences. Life is already serious enough as it is—a celebration of differences can even save a relationship!

COMMUNICATION TOOLS

In today's fast-paced world, we are expected to perform, respond, and communicate faster than ever before. The old rules of "business hours" rarely apply today. Today's expectations in communication are like a 24-hour drive-through—always open for business.

Eye contact has been replaced with screen contact, and voice communication has been replaced with texting; and it's now more important than ever before to be able to grab someone's attention with your communication quickly and effectively and know which medium to use for that situation.

Every text, e-mail, and phone call shapes your relationships. One wrong word can cost a tremendous amount of time, end an entire sale, damage a relationship, or upset a client. What we say and how, when, and where we say it will have a profound impact on the results we do or don't get.

In this section, I will introduce you to my four-step H.O.P.E. method and show you how you can create meaningful, powerful, and connected conversations. It's a method that teaches you how to use time with intention and enhance your relationships. It shows you how to communicate effectively to perform more with time and how to say no to protect your time.

Relational Communication: The H.O.P.E. Four-Step Process

"Relational communication" is about the exchange of energy (body language) and information (words) that allows for a mindful and relevant connection with others.

One of the relational communication tools I created is the H.O.P.E. four-step process to help my clients close any performance gaps in their communication. H.O.P.E. stands for *heart, outcome, personal interest,* and *enter their world.* The process is highly valuable for improving effectiveness and efficiency in communication while creating positive relationships among friends, coworkers, colleagues, and clients.

Let's examine each step in turn:

1. **HEART—Come from your heart.** Start by focusing your attention on your heart and asking yourself, "What is it that I want for me in this relationship (connection, trust, longevity)?" "What is it that I want others to have and feel in the relationship (connected, safe, open)?

   When we start from the heart, it can soften the grip of anxiety and stress and the need for control we often have and allow ourselves to be more empathetic and compassionate for ourselves and the person we are communicating with. It connects us to what really matters in the relationship.

2. **OUTCOME—What's the best possible outcome? For me? For others? For us as a team?** Be clear in your conversation what outcome you want. What do you want to happen or not happen for you? Then ask yourself, "What outcome do I want for the person I am communicating with? Or the team?"

   Each of these steps is creating the opportunity to walk in the shoes of others to better understand what their experience in this particular situation might be. The more perspective, flexibility, influence, and connection you have in your communication will translate into more confidence and comfort with your delivery. Plus, a better understanding of what matters most to them will allow you to collect additional relevant information that will help in the conversation.

3. **PERSONAL INTEREST—What's their personal interest and mine?** Personal interest is connected to more of the "why" of your outcome and theirs. "How will I benefit or what will I gain from this outcome, and how will this impact me personally and/or my business?"

   It is helpful to look at the big picture here with the 40,000-foot perspective of how your desired outcome connects to everything else. Next, do the same for others. What's their personal interest in this situation? How is that important to them and why? We often get caught up in focusing on just what *we* want. We need to speak clearly and directly to what's in it for them and then point out the shared benefits.

4. **ENTER THEIR WORLD—When, where, and how.** Entering their world has a few dimensions. First is determining when, where, and how to have the conversation—timing is everything. When is the best opportunity for your message to be heard most effectively? Depending on people's personality and style, this could dramatically affect the outcome of the conversation if you choose the wrong time. Make an appointment so they are pre-

pared and ready to engage. Is the conversation best face-to-face? On the phone? Through e-mail? These are the things to consider when setting up and engaging in the conversation for the best overall outcome.

The last step to prepare and ensure having a powerful conversation is to write down your thoughts for each step of the H.O.P.E. process. By writing them down, you will provide a script to follow, keeping you on track communicating your most important points for having the best possible conversation.

Your ability to communicate effectively in the workplace and personally has a profound impact on your time and how you perform with it. Here are my best strategies to stop saying yes to things you shouldn't spend your time on and maximize when and how long you engage with people.

OPENING AND CLOSING CONVERSATIONS

> If you want more time, freedom,
> and energy, start saying no.
> —Anonymous

Scheduling and presetting communication timelines and boundaries will get you back dozens of hours a month and improve the efficiency and effectiveness of your conversations (timing).

I find people are more concise when they have a time limitation and an understanding of what is expected on the phone or in person. Here are some examples of how I show my clients to finesse closing conversations:

- "Hi John, I saw it was you calling so I wanted to pick up. I only have five minutes right now, so if you need more time, we can schedule a call for later."

- "Hi Cindy, I'm calling you because I have some important information about your project that I wanted to deliver ASAP. I do want to be up front with you and tell you that I only have 10 minutes to review this with you before the team meeting. If that works for you, let's get started. We can schedule another call if needed."

I set a kitchen timer or my iPhone for a minute before the end of the call. This helps me avoid the urge to check the time, allowing me to be more engaged and present.

How to Say No

If there is one skill used wisely to reclaim and protect your time, it's the skill of saying *no*. With so many demands coming at us so fast, we can easily say yes and overcommit to things without taking the time to evaluate them. As Brené Brown shares in her book *Dare to Lead*, "Clear is kind, unclear is unkind."[1] When we say yes or no, we're being clear with ourselves and the people in our lives, which is an act of kindness that sets up clear boundaries and expectations with our time commitments.

Every request of your time is a request of your most precious resource and therefore must be treated accordingly. We simply apply the Time Cleanse Question that you now have—"Is this contributing or contaminating to my happiness and success?"

Now I'm not suggesting that you become completely self-centered. The key here is a healthy, balanced life that is of service but not to the detriment of your own well-being and purpose. Remember, your *no* is a supportive *yes* to your life and dreams and the antidote to not being hijacked by someone else's agenda.

Here are the steps on how to say no:

1. **PREPARE YOURSELF FOR CONSCIOUSLY SAYING NO.**
   Review for yourself why it's a no for you based on your values. Set up a procedure or rules for saying no. Examples:

   - "I have a rule or commitment with myself that (*x*)."

- "I have a rule with myself that I only go on two new client meetings a week."

- "I have a commitment to myself that I don't go out for dinner during the workweek, so I can wake up early to be at the gym at 6 a.m."

- "Saturdays are my recovery day, and I don't do anything before 3 p.m."

2. **PRACTICE SAYING NO OUT LOUD.** Practicing your no is important. If you wait to be in a situation under stress, without practice, there is a good chance you will default to a yes. Recording it is a good idea. I have my clients do this all the time, so they can hear how it sounds and they can deliver it with sincerity. Most people are shocked when they hear their voice tone or volume (it's usually not aligned with how they want to sound). Rehearsal adds considerable confidence.

3. **PAUSE, TAKE A BREATH, AND COUNT TO THREE.** Doing this gives you the space to disrupt the autopilot knee-jerk reaction that could potentially have you saying yes before you have gone through your decision-making steps. Remember, you are under no obligation to answer immediately. A simple "Thanks for asking. I'll consider it and get back to you later today (or tomorrow, or . . .)" is totally acceptable, and it is your time. Remember that before you obligate yourself, whenever appropriate, wait 24 hours to respond.

4. **HAVE "GO-TO" RESPONSES READY.** A few examples:

- "Thanks for asking. I would if I could, but it's not a good time for me with my workload."

- "Thanks, I appreciate your asking me, but my time is already committed."

- "I really appreciate your thinking about me for this, but my time is already committed."

- "I'm not available for that, but I can recommend someone who may be able to help you."

- "Here is what I can do . . ." Then limit the commitment to what will be comfortable for you.

- "I wish I could, but it's just not going to work right now."

- "I'll get back to you tomorrow."

Have Rehearsed Responses to Limit Conversation or Avoid Entering One

Having a strategy and a preloaded repertoire of responses to elegantly end conversations or avoid entering into them altogether is an absolute when it comes to protecting your time. Most people become so preoccupied in how to end a conversation that it keeps them from being fully engaged and getting the value out of the conversation they are in.

The suggestions below are both decisive and direct. Once you use these responses enough, they will become second nature.

Avoiding

1. "I'd love to stop and talk, but I have a meeting in five minutes."

2. "I'm late for a conference call."

3. "I've got to get home to the kids."

4. "I'm on deadline right now."

5. "I'm not feeling well right now. I need to go."

Ending

1. "It was great catching up, but it's time for me to get home now."

2. "It was a great meeting! I will see everyone later. I have to catch a train."

3. "I see a great opportunity here. I will follow up with you later."

4. "Thanks for taking the time to meet, but I have to go; my dogs are waiting for me."

5. "I'm not feeling well right now, so I need to go."

Who Does What by When

This next strategy has saved me and my clients thousands of hours of wasted time and has been key to improving results.

Whether it's an individual conversation or an extensive team meeting, most people get caught up in the excitement of opportunities or are bored out of their mind and want to move on to the next thing in their day or to-do list.

By slowing things down, this technique makes sure the time you just invested has a big return. Everyone on the call or at the meeting should know who's responsible for next steps and by when. Time commitments are for accelerating results and keeping a project moving and will protect against future redundant conversations.

Simply agreeing about who will be doing what by when will clearly set the direction of responsibilities with an agreed-upon timeline. How many times have you had a meeting and regrouped later to find out that no one is on the same page? Change that forever with this method.

Who (x) does what (y) by when (z).

EXAMPLE

Maja (x) is going to have the client reports complete to David (y) by noon June 26 (z).

If you'd like a formal worksheet for your meetings, I suggest the following, which you can download at www.timecleanse.com/book.

Meeting purpose and outcome:
Attending:
Notes:
Who does what:
By when:
Follow-up time to reconvene for next meeting:

Understanding Time Types and utilizing these communication strategies will help you relate to others, connect and engage effectively with yourself and others, improve your teamwork, save you hundreds of hours a year, and help direct your time to the things that are most important to you in creating greater and faster results.

CHAPTER 9

Setting Up Your Day to Perform

It's not the will to win that matters—everyone has that.
It's the will to prepare to win that matters.
—Paul "Bear" Bryant

PREPARATION LEADS TO SUCCESS. THIS IS THE SECRET of champions. They prepare to win every single day. How you prepare your day will determine the level of success you have on a daily, weekly, monthly, quarterly, and yearly basis.

In this chapter we want to cash in on your reclaimed time. By learning how to set your day to perform, you'll maximize your productivity with every hour of your day.

This chapter is broken into two sections. The first section will help you understand the best hours to perform based on your chronotype. The second section will teach you how to set up your day to get results faster, more consistently, and easier than ever before.

It's *go time*!

UNDERSTANDING YOU!

Performance Scheduling

> Success is simple. Do what's right,
> the right way, at the right time.
> —Arnold Glasow

Performance scheduling is about doing the right thing at the right time. A big part of the Time Cleanse is *what to do* and *what not to do* at any given time. Utilizing your performance schedule, you can focus on *when to do what* to maximize your best time for performance.

Our internal clock dictates the rhythm of our energy throughout the day, affecting our focus and motivation at various times. Many people have the right intentions and are doing the right things but at the wrong time. Having the right conversation at the wrong time with a loved one or colleague; attempting to exercise when you are tired and your body is not ready; trying to solve a creative problem when you are too tired to concentrate or generate sales when you're distracted—all these situations can be frustrating or a losing battle just because the *timing* is off.

Each of us has a "chronotype," or personal pattern of circadian rhythms, that influences our physiology and psychology. Daniel Pink offers his insight on this in his book *When: The Scientific Secrets of Perfect Timing*.[1] He explains that human beings don't all experience the day in precisely the same way. *When* we do things does matter: "It's not more important than 'what,' 'how,' or 'who,' but it's as important," says Pink.

There are two main chronotypes:

1. The *Lark* (or *Early Bird*) wakes up and goes to bed early.

2. The *Owl* (or *Night Owl*) wakes up and goes to bed late.

All people generally experience their day in three stages (with some variances):

1. **PEAK.** When we perform at our best

2. **LULL.** When we feel a drop in our physical or mental energy

3. **RECOVERY.** When we feel good enough to perform at a high level again

Understanding when these happen in *your* day will determine if you are an Early Bird or Night Owl.

According to research, about 75 percent of people feel the *peak* in the morning, the *lull* in the afternoon, and the *recovery* in the evening. These are the Early Birds.[2]

The other 25 percent of the population feel the opposite. They experience the *recovery* first in the morning, the *lull* in energy in the afternoon, and then their highest level of energy, or *peak*, in the evening. These people are the Night Owls.

So if you're an Early Bird, your most demanding mental or physical tasks should be scheduled and accomplished in the morning, and if you're a Night Owl, those same tasks should be scheduled and done later in the day or in the evening.

Knowing and activating your best personal performance hours is critical in maximizing your day.

Daniel Pink suggests that you align your activities to maximize your day with your chronotype in the following ways:

If You Are an Early Bird . . .

- **MORNING.** Do things in the morning that require more alertness. This includes making decisions, writing important reports and memos, and having critical conversations.

- **MIDDAY.** Do things that require less focus and are low-demand tasks, for example, scheduling and organizing.

- **LATE AFTERNOON/EVENING.** This is a good time for creative endeavors and brainstorming, as well as doing morning activities if the energy is there for it.

If You Are a Night Owl . . .

- **MORNING.** This is a good time for creative endeavors and brainstorming.

- **MIDDAY.** Do things that require less focus and are low-demand tasks, such as scheduling, organizing, etc.

- **LATE AFTERNOON/EVENING.** Do things that require more alertness, such as decision making, critical conversations, and cognitive tasks.

It's important to remember that these suggestions are a guide, and people have their own unique biology. Understanding your specific energy flow, focus, and attention throughout the day allows you to personalize what you do and when for your best performance.

To help you with tracking and determining your best hours, I've created a simple worksheet for you that can be downloaded at www.timecleanse.com/book. This is a valuable chronobiology tool that will help you evaluate the patterns of your day and account for your time and activities after completing the entire Time Cleanse process.

SETTING UP YOUR DAY

> Make every day your masterpiece.
> —John Wooden

Setting up your day consists of three parts:

1. **BEFORE (PREPARATION).** This is getting you started in your day preparing your mind and body in a positive way.

2. **DURING (PERFORMING).** This is performing and keeping your focus and energy at optimal levels.

3. **AFTER (RECOVERY).** This is recovering from the day and recharging for the next.

Before

As soon as you're awake or your alarm goes off, your day starts. This is your "before" time. This is an important part of your day because how you start your day sets the tone for how you engage and perform for the rest of the time you are awake.

The best way to start your day off right is to get up immediately. This sets your mindset for positive action, momentum, and for taking charge of your day.

I know many people have a hard time getting out of bed and delay it by hitting the snooze button. I like Mel Robbins's technique to overcome this. In her book *The 5 Second Rule*, she suggests counting down from 5, and by the time you get to 1, you are taking action. Robbins says this creates an activation energy and momentum. I use it and train my clients to do it, and it works.[3]

A technique to keep that momentum going comes from Admiral William McRaven's book *Make Your Bed*.[4] He shares the 10 lessons he learned from Navy SEAL training that can change the world, like making your bed. He explains, "Nothing can replace the strength and comfort of one's faith, but sometimes the simple act of making your bed can give you the lift you need to start your day and provide you the satisfaction to end it right."

For the last 15 years of my life, making my bed right after I wake up has been my daily practice. It allows me to begin each day feeling accomplished, and having an environment that's clean and organized sets my intention in a positive way for the day.

There are three main keys to start your day right:

1. Know and review your three top priorities.

2. Set your intentions connected to your three priorities.

3. Spend time in personal reflection to connect with your inner self (for example: meditation, prayer, contemplation, etc.).

Here is my morning routine:

My Before Routine

1. Get up when my alarm goes off.

2. Immediately make my bed.

3. Engage in a time of silence for myself, which includes 20 minutes of meditation.

4. Review my top three priorities for the day (these are set the night before, as you will see at the end of the chapter).

5. Set intentions for each of my three priorities.

6. Exercise for one hour.

7. Have a cup of coffee.

I schedule my Before routine this way:

4 a.m.	
4:30	
5 a.m.	Get up when my alarm goes off and immediately make my bed.
5:30	Do 20 minutes of meditation.
6 a.m.	Review my top three priorities for the day and set intentions for each of the three priorities.
6:30	Go to the gym.
7 a.m.	
7:30	
8 a.m.	Have Bulletproof coffee and start my workday.

SETTING UP YOUR DAY TO PERFORM   **175**

In the space provided, write in your own Before routine.

4 a.m.	
4:30	
5 a.m.	
5:30	
6 a.m.	
6:30	
7 a.m.	
7:30	
8 a.m.	

During

> The path to success is to take massive,
> determined action.
> —TONY ROBBINS

"During" is the time of the day when you're performing and keeping your focus and energy at optimal levels. The following are key performance strategies, tools, and tips to maximize and maintain your time, productivity, and performance during this peak period of the day.

E-mail

E-mail is one of the biggest distractions we face in the workplace today. Most people do not have a strategy for this constant attention grabber, which causes interruptions and consumes time. The following are simple strategies that master your e-mail time and bring focus to your work.

1. Turn all notifications off, both auditory and visual. Doing this will help keep you focused and on track with what you're working on and not take you off course.

2. Plan ahead of time when you are going to check and answer e-mail. This is crucial, and you must keep to this commitment. For example, you can pick a time to check your e-mail at 8 a.m., 12, and/or 5 p.m.

3. Set a timer to check e-mail and train yourself to efficiently send and respond to all your e-mails in that time frame. If your job requires you to check your e-mail more frequently, set your timer to shorter increments and stick to it.

4. Set up a folder for e-mails that may require more time to respond or that can wait until the end of your day. Schedule a specific time for these types of e-mails and tackle at once.

Use Work/Rest Intervals

Work and rest intervals are a great way to train your brain for performance. In my experience, this tool allows you to have three to five times more productivity by having an uninterrupted hour where you can be completely focused.

For myself, I find that 55 minutes of work and 7 to 10 minutes of rest are ideal intervals of time. I use a kitchen timer (I don't use my iPhone, which could be a distraction) that I set for 55 minutes and then reset for 7 to 10 minutes to rest. After three rounds, I take a 30-minute break to recharge. It's important in this 30-minute break that you're engaging in something that allows you to recover, not jumping on social media sites or doing other distracting activities. Instead, I use my rest period to listen to music, take a walk outside, have something to eat, or quietly rest with my eyes closed.

Another specific technique you can use is the Pomodoro technique. This works in a similar way to work/rest intervals, but it differs in that it's specifically set at 25 minutes of work and 5 minutes of break time. After three rounds, you can take a longer break of 15 to 20 minutes. Then resume regular intervals and repeat.

No matter what strategy you use, it's important that you determine a period of time you'll be working and a period when you'll be taking a break that will work with your chronotype, individual style, and environment. Remember: Your breaks are just as important as your work periods. It allows you to continue working at optimal levels throughout the day.

Cluster

When reviewing the tasks for your day, look at how you can "cluster" similar activities together. The brain likes similar tasks, because it can perform in a more effective and efficient manner. So when you plan your day, see where you can group similar tasks together. Over a week's time you will see a major shift in how much you get done, as well as having more energy throughout the day.

Here's an example of how I cluster tasks in my day:

- **9:00–9:15:** Only e-mails

- **10:00–12:00:** Coaching calls

- **1:00–1:30:** Answering all team questions

The Eisenhower Matrix

The Eisenhower matrix is an effective old-school technique that has great value today. Developed by President Dwight D. Eisenhower to aid his decision-making process, this matrix helps you determine and prioritize your tasks according to their timing requirements and importance.[5] This matrix is key to making critical decisions in your day about where to invest your time.

Figure 9.1 depicts the matrix. The process for using it is simple, as it is based on whether a task is urgent or not urgent and important or not important. As you can see, each of the four quadrants forming the matrix represents a different choice:

1. **DO.** Tasks that require immediate attention:
   - These are urgent and important.
   - These are time-sensitive tasks that must be handled immediately.
   - These tasks should be prioritized according to level of importance and impact and should be scheduled accordingly.

2. **DECIDE.** Tasks that can be attended to later:
   - These are important but not urgent.

- While these tasks need to be done, they aren't time sensitive and can be rescheduled to accommodate the *do* tasks.

3. **DELEGATE.** Tasks that someone else can handle:

   - These are urgent but not important.

   - These tasks don't require your time, effort, and input and can be handled by someone else just as effectively, thereby freeing your time to concentrate on *do* tasks.

4. **DELETE.** Tasks that can be discarded:

   - These are not urgent or important.

   - After careful evaluation, these are mostly tasks that can be eliminated altogether.

As you work with the Eisenhower matrix, try to limit yourself to no more than eight tasks per quadrant. This will ensure that you complete tasks while also leaving room for unexpected events and unplanned tasks.

	Urgent	Not Urgent
Important	**DO** *Do it now.* Example: Schedule team meeting for today.	**DECIDE** *Set the meeting for that morning.* Example: Check company calendar for appropriate times.
Not Important	**DELEGATE** *Have Executive Assistant handle scheduling.* Example: E-mail immediately and provide agenda for the meeting.	**DELETE** *Consider alternate day for the meeting.* Example: Review company calendar and individual team schedules.

Figure 9.1   The Eisenhower matrix

It's important that the matrix include both your personal and your business tasks. By doing this, you'll be able to prioritize and integrate all the important aspects of your life.

Finally, you can use the matrix for yourself, your family, and/or your business. It's important to remember when using the matrix for yourself to not let others determine your priorities, their perceived level of importance, and the use of your time.

Limit Time with the News

Keeping up with the media and news is one of the most hypnotic, time-wasting activities available to distract you and capture your attention. Of course, staying up to date with current local and world affairs is important, but our curiosity or apparent addiction to constantly being "in the know" keeps us distracted and unproductive.

Most news stories are designed to trigger a fear response that keeps you primed for wanting more. At times, such as during a weather crisis in your area affecting your immediate travel path, that can be essential.

It's not useful for your daily productivity and performance to constantly be inundated with negativity. A good option is to get your news from online sources you trust and set a time limit beforehand. This way you can be in control of the news you consume and not get caught in the sensationalism of the news anchor presenting it.

Limit or Shut Off Notifications

While completely shutting down your smartphone or computer isn't always practical, managing your notifications is. Frequent pop-ups are distracting and overstimulating, so put your phone in airplane mode, so that e-mail or text messages don't distract you in times where you need to be focused.

Turn off all instant messages, text, Facebook, news, and other feeds that pop up on any and all of your screens.

Unsubscribe and Unfollow

If a newsletter or Twitter feed isn't providing you with value, unsubscribe or unfollow immediately. Just because it was something that interested you previously doesn't mean it's still relevant now. Cleaning up your inbox and feed will result in finding helpful information faster and reduce the time you spend maintaining your inbox. Repeat the process regularly for optimal effect.

Invest in More Screen Space

Research shows that having more screen space increases productivity. Having two full-size computer screens or a large single monitor can be incredibly beneficial for productivity. If you need to view two or more documents at a time, the ability to view multiple windows simultaneously eases the effort and minimizes the distraction of switching from one document to the next.

While writing this book, I regularly needed three or four documents open at the same time, so I invested in a LG 38-inch-wide screen to accommodate that. The larger screen made reading text easier and prevented me from constantly switching between pages or applications. That saved me hundreds of hours writing this book.

Standing Desk

If you spend multiple hours at your desk, your body can become fatigued and restricted, resulting in decreased productivity and reduced energy. Alternating sitting and standing throughout the day keeps both the body and the brain engaged, while keeping your energy flowing and motivating your mind to stay focused.

In one 7-week study from the Centers for Disease Control and Prevention, researchers found that participants using standing desks reported less stress and fatigue than those who remained seated the entire workday. Additionally, 87 percent of those using standing desks reported increased vigor and energy throughout the day.[6]

I schedule my During routine this way:

8 a.m.	
8:30	Coaching calls with standing desk
9 a.m.	Coaching calls
9:30	Coaching calls
10 a.m.	Coaching calls
10:30	
11 a.m.	Break—30-minute walk outside
11:30	E-mails
12 p.m.	Coaching team 1 hour
12:30	
1 p.m.	Eat meal—30 minutes
1:30	
2 p.m.	Meetings
2:30	Meetings
3 p.m.	Meetings
3:30	Meetings
4 p.m.	Break—meditation 20 minutes
4:30	
5 p.m.	Client phone calls
5:30	Client phone calls
6 p.m.	End of workday
6:30	

Now write in your own schedule (points to consider: work/rest interval, breaks, clustering, etc., when filling out).

8 a.m.	
8:30	
9 a.m.	
9:30	
10 a.m.	
10:30	
11 a.m.	
11:30	
12 p.m.	
12:30	
1 p.m.	
1:30	
2 p.m.	
2:30	
3 p.m.	
3:30	
4 p.m.	
4:30	
5 p.m.	
5:30	
6 p.m.	
6:30	

After

> Preparation for tomorrow is hard work today.
> —BRUCE LEE

I consider "after" the time when you complete your regular workday until the time you go to sleep. I have broken down this time frame into two parts.

Part I is the two to fours hours following work. These few hours are neglected by most people and spent wasted in front of the TV or online.

Your "after" hours are a powerful time to invest in things that matter most. It's your time to engage with family and friends, invest in your personal growth, learn a language, read, improve your business knowledge, or even volunteer for a cause you believe in. This prime time can be used for anything that makes you happy and advances who you are.

Be sure you make the most of it.

Part II of your evening or the hour before sleep focuses on reviewing your day and preparation for the next day. Here are two important things to do in preperation for your next day.

Define Your Three

The "power of three" technique forces you to focus on three things that will make the biggest difference in your day.

In his book *Getting Results the Agile Way*, J. D. Meier suggests the following steps to put this into action:[7]

1. Write down three things you want to accomplish *today*.

2. Write down three things you want to accomplish *this week*.

3. Write down three things you want to achieve *this year*.

Meier asserts that the problem with a lot of productivity and time management systems is that they require a lot of overhead, but the *rule of three* doesn't. Every morning you think about the main three things you have to do, and then you do them. It's a great technique to figure out what you need to focus on.

The reason you should pick three is that our brain has been trained to think in threes and can focus well on that number. We know our ABCs; ready, set, go; gold, silver, bronze; and so on.

Establishing your top three the night before will allow you to be ready and focused right from the start of your day.

Schedule Everything

Now that you have established your three top priorities, it's time to schedule what you need to do to accomplish them. You can do this successfully by making sure you put your tasks on your calendar. Your calendar is where you are committing your most valuable asset (time) to your most valuable priorities. If your tasks are not on your calendar with the appropriate time scheduled for them, there is a good chance they won't happen.

Your daily schedule should be the written and visual reminder of what you have chosen to do on any given day, which guides the intentions you set for every day. It represents what's important in your life and business. There is an old productivity saying I live by: "If it's not on the calendar, it didn't happen." Live with this mindset and calendar everything that is important.

Here is my After schedule:

6:30	
7 p.m.	Read
7:30	Do research for my book
8 p.m.	Spend time with my girlfriend 8–10
8:30	
9 p.m.	
9:30	
10 p.m.	Fill out the Complete the Day Worksheet
10:30	Go to sleep
11 p.m.	
11:30	

Now fill in your personal After schedule:

6:30	
7 p.m.	
7:30	
8 p.m.	
8:30	
9 p.m.	
9:30	
10 p.m.	
10:30	
11 p.m.	
11:30	

Complete the Day Worksheet

The following Complete the Day Worksheet is an essential tool for processing and decompressing after your day. Completing this worksheet every day will help you analyze and evaluate your daily performance, bring clarity and direction, as well as prepare you to perform for the next day.

These instructions will help you complete the worksheet.

Today

1. Write down your top three successes, big or small, that you had during your day. The important thing is to acknowledge what went well.

2. Write down any challenges you faced during the day so that you can recognize and process them.

3. Make a list of tools you can utilize in the future to overcome those challenges (for example, 4-7-8 breathing, head-heart-body, reset strategy, etc. (These strategies are described in Chapter 10.)

4. Rewind your day by closing your eyes and replaying your day from the moment you woke up to where you are right now. Notice anything you would have liked to happen differently; then visualize your day starting over again and going the way you want it to go. This technique reinforces and programs in the right strategies to use going forward.

5. Lastly, write down three things you're grateful for. Doing so helps you end the day on a positive note.

Next Day

1. Now that you've gone through today, it's time to prepare for the next day. Begin by listing the three priorities you want to focus on for tomorrow.

2. Decide on your intention for the day that will reinforce your top three priorities for the day.

3. Write down any performance tools you're focused on using throughout your day.

COMPLETE THE DAY WORKSHEET

Date:

TODAY

1. **Top three successes:**

   1. _____
   2. _____
   3. _____

2. **Challenges:**

   _____
   _____
   _____

3. **What tools can I use to overcome these challenges?**

   _____
   _____

4. **Rewind my day with "How I wanted it to be."**

5. **What am I grateful for in my life?**

   1. _____
   2. _____
   3. _____

NEXT DAY

6. **Top three goals/priorities:**

   _____
   _____
   _____

7. **What is my intention for my priorities?**

   _____
   _____
   _____

8. **What performance enhancement tools will I use?**

   _____
   _____
   _____

Weekly and Monthly Review Worksheets

Now that you've learned how to fill out your Complete the Day Worksheet, it's time to move on to two more worksheets to review your weekly and monthly performance.

By filling out your weekly and monthly performance review sheets, you will learn to evaluate your performance on a regular basis in order to make continual adjustments and improvements to maximize your full potential. All the worksheets in this chapter are available for download at www.timecleanse.com/book.

Weekly Review Worksheet

At the end of each week, fill out your Weekly Review Worksheet that can be found on page 188. Follow the instructions below to monitor and make adjustments to your performance:

1. Circle the level of satisfaction you have from your week.

2. Write down your top three (or more) successes.

3. Write down lessons you learned this week.

4. Write down what your biggest challenge was for this week and how you will overcome it.

5. Are there any improvements you can make with the use of your time?

6. How present and timeful were you during the week (with 1 being the least satisfied and 10 being the most satisfied)?

7. Write down the three things you are most grateful for in your life.

WEEKLY REVIEW WORKSHEET

1. **Circle my level of satisfaction with this week**
   (with 1 being the least satisfied and 10 being the most satisfied):

1	2	3	4	5	6	7	8	9	10

2. **What were my three (or more) biggest successes this week?**

1. _____
2. _____
3. _____

3. **What were the three biggest lessons I learned this week?**

1. _____
2. _____
3. _____

4. **What was my biggest challenge of this week?**
   How will I overcome this challenge (tools I have)?

1. _____
2. _____
3. _____

5. **Are there any improvements I can make with the use of my time?**

_____
_____
_____
_____

6. **How present and timeful was I during the week**
   (with 1 being the least satisfied and 10 being the most satisfied)?

1	2	3	4	5	6	7	8	9	10

7. **What are the three things I am most grateful for in my life?**

_____
_____
_____

Monthly Review Worksheet

I highly recommend not just evaluating each week, but each month at month's end as well. By taking a look at the larger monthly picture in addition to your weekly reviews, you will see what you've accomplished over a longer time period, which will allow you to see patterns of energy, focus, and performance you can capitalize on.

MONTHLY REVIEW WORKSHEET

1. Circle my level of satisfaction with this month
   (with 1 being the least satisfied and 10 being the most satisfied):

1	2	3	4	5	6	7	8	9	10

2. What were my three biggest successes this month?

   1. _____
   2. _____
   3. _____

3. What were the three biggest lessons I learned this last month?

   1. _____
   2. _____
   3. _____

4. What was my biggest challenge of this month?
   How will I overcome this challenge (tools I have)?

   1. _____
   2. _____
   3. _____

5. Are there any improvements I can make with the use of my time?
   Specific action items:

   _____
   _____
   _____
   _____

6. How present and timeful was I during during the month (in the moment)
   (with 1 being the least satisfied and 10 being the most satisfied)?

1	2	3	4	5	6	7	8	9	10

7. How and where have I improved from the previous month?

   _____
   _____
   _____
   _____

To continue your performance improvement, save all your worksheets, whether electronically or in a binder. Not only will this allow you to easily and periodically review your performance, it will serve as a reminder for all you have accomplished over the weeks and months of your life.

By taking the time to prepare and ensure you perform effectively with your day, you will see lasting results. The minutes you spend planning your day will save you hours and increase your performance and productivity. Your results will skyrocket, and you will see more money, happiness, and success in your business and life.

CHAPTER

10

Time Performance Tools, Tactics, and Tips

No whining. No complaining. No excuses.
—ANGELA DUCKWORTH

THE ONE THING WE ALL WANT IS PERFORMANCE—
action, execution, achievement, accomplishment. Yes, all of this and more
makes up performance. I'm sure it's one of the big reasons you picked up
this book.

As you know by now, my philosophy for you is not just about performance, but about how to perform with time to get the fastest results possible, making great memories, having fun, and enjoying the process along
the way.

For over 25 years I've been entrusted by top-performing executives,
CEOs, entrepreneurs, military leaders, pro athletes, and celebrities to help
them achieve optimal performance. In this chapter, I will share my top
tools, tactics, tips, and strategies for you to do more, get more, and be more
in less time.

HAVE AN INTERRUPTION RESET STRATEGY

One of the biggest blind spots people have that impact their performance
is not being prepared in how to handle interruptions during their day.

Interruptions are going to happen; we all know that. But how you handle these interruptions can be the difference between success and failure. Having a strategy for times when things go off track will ensure your consistent performance no matter what life throws at you.

When we look at our days, there is always something that comes up that was unplanned, from common interruptions to regular distractions and full-blown crises. In my coaching, I regularly see individuals at all levels in organizations make one critical mistake that can be devastating to their daily productivity and performance: They don't have a strategy for when things go off track to reset their high-performance state. They seemed surprised or even shocked when they've been derailed and often use the excuse that because something unexpected happened, they couldn't accomplish what they'd planned because they didn't have enough time.

The truth is that something unexpected happens every day. When people get distracted, either it takes a long time to get back on track, or the rest of the day gets completely lost for anything productive. The important thing here is to understand that interruptions and distractions happen, to not get discouraged, and to have a preset strategy to reset yourself. The highest-performing people know how to get back on track fast when they're off course.

Three-Step Reset Strategy: Recognize-Repair-Reengage

This three-step strategy will put you back on the right track:

Step 1. Recognize

You need to be aware that you are off course and no longer focused on your daily plan and schedule. A technique I learned for this comes from Chris Bailey, the author of *Hyperfocus*,[1] which is to set what he calls an "awareness chime," an alarm on your phone every hour to check in to where your awareness is when the chime goes off and where it has been the last hour. This is an incredibly powerful tool to build the mental muscle of awareness by developing the habit of checking in with your focus on an hourly basis.

For example, when you check in, you recognize that a meeting that was planned for 30 minutes took more than an hour and now has you behind for the rest of your day.

Step 2. Repair

Now that you're aware that you're off track, it's time to repair your day by evaluating what you need to shift, change, or alter to accomplish what's most important. By evaluating what's in front of you, it may be appropriate to cancel or reschedule less urgent items and redirect your energy and focus to the most important tasks for the rest of the day. For example, you may reschedule your lunchtime workout for the end of the day or reschedule a nonessential team meeting for another day.

The important thing here is to not try to compress what you prescheduled into the amount of time left in your day, e.g., compress your schedule that legitimately requires three hours of engagement into one hour. Make adjustments that support your productivity and performance, not compromise them.

Step 3. Reengage

Reengaging focuses you on getting your mind and body back to your best performance state. This might require that you reset or refocus yourself by utilizing any of the following techniques individually or in combination: meditation, visualization, head-heart-body, 4-7-8 breathing, 5-minute walk, and circle of excellence (all these are described later in this chapter).

Here's an example of a reset strategy in action: You *realize* you have spent the last 30 minutes looking at new car models online. Now that you recognize you're off course with your schedule, you *repair* it by canceling the 30 minutes you were going to spend at the nearby coffee shop for lunch. You then *reengage* by doing a series of 4-7-8 breaths or taking a 5-minute break to reset yourself back to your best performance state and get you back on track for the rest of your day.

TECHNOLOGY AND PERFORMANCE

In the thousands of presentations I've delivered and with the clients I've trained, there is mass confusion about technology and how to use it effectively. Somewhere along the way, we started to believe that technology would be the great savior of time and allow us to have more freedom and productivity. But to our surprise, what happened instead was that we increased the drive to do more in less time—which then led to often doing more than one thing at a time. As demands increased, so did the devices we used to get things done.

With multiple demands and multiple devices, we became addicted to the stimulation, and we've trained ourselves to often not be in the moment because of switching back and forth from one thing to the next.

We now find it very hard to stay focused or get the most out of any moment because our brains are addicted to stimulating distraction, constantly trying to take us away from what matters most. Our best effort to keep up has led us to living a life of multitasking.

All this distraction and overstimulation is stealing our focus, as well as costing us time, money, and loss in productivity. Because of this, our lives today are being ruled and driven by the belief that multitasking is the only way to survive in our personal lives and in business.

MINDFUL MULTITASKING

Our brains best respond when we focus on a single task. Many believe they are actually multitasking, but in reality, they are "task switching," which means that they're repeatedly switching their focus from one task to another for brief periods of time. For many people, those brief periods of time become their entire day.

To make you aware of the difference, here are a couple examples of true multitasking: riding a stationary bike and listening to an audiobook at the same time; folding clothes while talking to your friend on the phone. Both of these examples show that you can effectively do two things at once while also being engaged, because they are habits or require very low attention.

This type of multitasking can actually be very beneficial in the use of your time when you're doing low-level, low-attention, habitual activities.

What we're focused on here going forward is multitasking in the context of task switching. I know, many people think they are "great at multitasking." But the Time Cleanse is going to expose multitasking, in its traditional form, as the time and productivity stealer that it is.

The University of California at Irvine studied multitasking and found that "the typical office worker is interrupted or switches tasks, on average, every three minutes and five seconds." And that "it takes an average of 23 minutes and 15 seconds to get back to the task."[2]

Additionally, a study at the University of London found that we lose as many as 10 IQ points when trying to multitask,[3] and research conducted at Stanford found that multitasking affected memory and people were less productive than when doing a single thing at a time.[4]

Multitasking creates the illusion that we're getting more done, and that makes us feel good mainly because of the feel-good chemical, dopamine, that's released. We end up with more activity, less productivity, and decreased quality of work. We clearly know one thing from the research: As good as it may feel, multitasking does not improve performance.

While the ability to multitask is supposed to be a skill that increases productivity and saves time, it really steals time from you in ways you probably don't even realize, including:

- Makes you less efficient

- Reduces your focus

- Impairs the quality of experience

- Negatively impacts your overview

- Increases mistakes

- Creates a negative habit

- Trains your brain to seek stimulation and distraction

- Hinders your ability to enter a "flow state"

So what do we do? We multitask mindfully. Mindful multitasking is being present in the moment by being consciously aware as you switch from task to task.

Mindful multitasking prepares you and creates awareness that in this period of time, you'll be switching from one thing to another. In that process, you'll be consciously aware as you shift from task to task. It is in the awareness and in the switching where the benefits of mindfulness can be activated and engaged, allowing you to maximize your time and productivity versus the old, traditional way of multitasking without awareness.

Continuing with this mindset of being aware that you're switching will ultimately create an environment of being present in task switching. Over time, this will develop into a skill of being mindful in your multitasking.

By practicing mindful multitasking, you will find there is more efficiency, meaning, and structure in your day. When you are more present, you will begin to reset and reconnect to the intention behind your action, reducing the traditional negative effects of multitasking.

Steps to Take to Mindfully Multitask

You must continue to recognize that effective multitasking is *not* doing two things at once. It's being truly present while switching focus back and forth between tasks. You are being conscious of your first task only, and when additional tasks require you to switch focus, being mindful, you consciously shift to the next task.

There are three steps to mindful multitasking:

STEP 1. Consider why you are multitasking. Be conscious of the decision to multitask (task switch) and proceed with the intention and purpose behind it. Although you are now mindfully multitasking, be aware that you're still focusing on more than one thing and that will affect your overall productivity and performance. Being conscious of this will keep you from entering into higher-stake or higher-value situations that may end up costing you in the long run, e.g., work that has to be redone, poor communication, lack of quality production, etc.

STEP 2. Choose activities that have low value and low consequence versus high-stakes conversations or interactions.

STEP 3. Set clear goals and time limits on multitasking (speed multitasking, as I call it, can be very effective by setting short time periods of 10 to 20 minutes). By having a conscious start and stop time, you'll be most effective with your mindful multitasking.

Here are the positive changes you will see as you begin to integrate mindful multitasking:

OLD WAY	MINDFUL
Not aware	Aware
Not present	Present
React	Respond
No time limits	Set time limits
Single focused	Overall awareness
Switching	Shifting
Automatic	Conscious choice
Out of control	In control
Creates stress	Decreases stress
Generates mistakes	Less mistakes
Decreases productivity	Increases productivity and performance

By utilizing mindful multitasking, you will enjoy the benefits of having more time for what matters most in your life.

Mindfully Managing Technology in Action

Now let's see how to manage your technology in real life. Below are some common scenarios my clients face, along with guidelines on how you can shift to being mindful with your technology.

Kid's Event

When you know you are going to be unavailable because you are at an event for your child, let anyone affected know. Anticipate and wrap up outstanding urgent items, texts, e-mails, calls, and so on in preparation for this event. These simple steps will reduce anxiety and stress during the event while you are off your technology.

Spend three minutes consciously shifting gears to be present and fully engaged (whether that's through breathing, meditation, or self-talk). Let go of the other demands competing for your attention and energy and be fully present at your child's event. Your presence has an impact on the experience and activity of those around you. The difference between them seeing you texting and you actively watching and encouraging them can be far more important than their own performance and the outcome of the event.

DO: Put your phone on vibrate or shut it off and place it out of sight. Set aside time after the event to get caught up on texts, e-mails, calls, etc.

DON'T: Look at or use your phone to text, check social media, or take calls during the event.

Dinner

Knowing you are going to be out of pocket for the next two hours, let anyone affected know that you will be unavailable. Anticipate and wrap up outstanding urgent items, texts, e-mails, calls, and so on, as you learned in the previous example.

DO: Engage in conversations and interactions without electronics. If you are going to take pictures or show someone a video or picture, determine a time for this, such as between the main course and dessert, and set time limits. If you absolutely have to use your phone, excuse yourself and go to the lobby or outside so you don't interrupt the conversation at the table. Remember why you are there at that dinner and be present to the benefits and rewards of being in the company of these particular people.

DON'T: Put your phone on the table, answer calls, text, or post on social media during dinner.

In the Car

We spend so much time in the car, and it is so easy to get charmed into using our devices. But think about all that's at stake, whether you are driving or are a passenger—it's time to engage in things other than your device. We all are aware of the huge cost of distracted driving in the rise of accidents.

DO: Pay attention to your surroundings. Engage in conversation when others are in the car with you. If alone, listen to audiobooks or music, or simply enjoy the quiet.

DON'T: Text or talk on the phone, even hands-free. Research shows that even a hands-free call impairs your reaction equal to the effects of one or two alcohol drinks.

Walking

Pedestrian accidents massively increase when individuals are wearing earbuds or headsets as situational awareness is reduced.

DO: Stay alert and engaged in your surroundings.

DON'T: Look at your phone or text while walking. Don't walk with earbuds in or engage in a conversation on your phone that distracts you from your surroundings.

Meetings

Research shows that just having your phone out where it can be seen can reduce the effectiveness of meetings.

DO: Schedule a specific time and duration for each meeting. Be an active listener, make eye contact with anyone who is speaking, and take notes. If you have to use your phone or computer, be sure to turn off your notifications. At the end of the meeting, make sure everyone knows who is doing what and by when. If you aren't clear, ask for clarification. If you need to schedule a follow-up or continuation meeting, do so.

DON'T: Text, e-mail, or use social media during meetings. Don't have your phone out. Just seeing it interrupts your train of thought and steals your focus unless you are using it to take notes.

Vacation

When it comes to taking vacations, preparation is key. You don't want your time off to turn into a "workcation" where you'll be splitting your focus between work and relaxation and play, and you won't return refreshed and rested.

DO: Handle all items personally and professionally before you leave, and if there is overflow that can't be completed before you leave, either competently delegate it or let the appropriate people know you will be gone and when to expect a follow-up upon your return. If you absolutely must work during vacation, set aside specific times to do so and return to vacation mode when that time is ended.

DON'T: Check e-mail and texts in a random or impromptu way. Free time should remain free time—not an opportunity to check in with work.

WAYS TO BUY YOUR TIME BACK

As you learned earlier in the book, research shows that buying back your time increases happiness. The following services, covering a variety of areas, can save you countless hours so that you can focus your time on what matters most to you.

Use a Car Service

Uber and Lyft have been a game changer for me and my clients. A car service is a valuable tool to maximize your time and productivity. By having someone else get you from point A to point B, you make time to conduct sales calls, write reports, plan projects, follow up with clients, and arrive rested. This is a serious consideration to increase your productivity.

Shop Online

Online shopping platforms such as Amazon, which is one of my favorites, provide immense savings in shopping time. As an early adopter of Amazon since 2007, I have been using it for years, and it has saved me hundreds of hours of travel and shopping time. You can have everything from office supplies to clothing and food delivered to your door the same day you order.

Make Use of Services to Do Tasks and Errands

You can use services such as NeedTo, TaskRabbit, and Handy to hire people to do tasks or errands. Anything from packing and moving, to home improvement projects, handyman services, and more, is available.

Purchase Preselected Meals

Utilizing food prep and delivery services allows you to save shopping, travel, and cooking time. You'd be surprised how much time is saved when you calculate how much time it takes to create your own meals. Some food delivery services include Send a Meal, Freshly, Prepped, and Blue Apron.

Use Technology to Be Productive

Your phone, computer, and tablet can help you to be more productive in various ways. Here are some of my favorite apps. They can help you be more efficient, speed up your results, and make huge gains in productivity.

1. **GOAL SETTING.** Write down your goals for relationships, finances, career, health, and wellness in a place you can see them to remind you where you are spending your time and ensure the right focus. My favorite app for this is GoalsOnTrack.

2. **SOCIAL MEDIA WEBSITE RESTRICTION.** Use resources like http://www.Rescuetime.com to cut social media time in half. Meaningless scrolling on the internet can be a major time-waster for most people. The RescueTime app is a time management program that will monitor what you do on a computer and will provide a daily report of your productivity.

3. **TIMERS.** Create time limits for the things you do and time you spend on Facebook, phone calls, conversations with friends, Netflix, etc., by setting a timer to protect the hours that would have been lost. Most phones now include an app like this.

4. **UNSUBSCRIBE TOOL.** Unroll.Me is a simple app that hunts down all your subscriptions so you can look at them in a single e-mail, unsubscribe from unwanted lists, or ignore the e-mail and keep it "as is."

5. **TACKLING E-MAIL OVERWHELM.** Sanebox, http://www.sanebox.com/, is a third-party program that works with all e-mail clients. Its purpose is to only allow important messages to show up in your inbox. The rest are sent to a separate folder. Then, at the end of the day, or at another time you specify, it will send you a message that contains everything in the separate folder.

6. **AUTORESPONSE.** Gmail.com and other e-mail services have a tool for creating "canned responses" for common questions. You can use this to decrease the amount of communication you do through e-mail.

7. **ORGANIZING AND MANAGING.** Evernote is a handy and versatile app that can save your documents and notes (audio and

text), organize your photos, set reminders, upload attachments, and sync all your apps across your various desktop and mobile devices. Plus, Evernote's bookmark feature makes it easy to clip web articles and store them for later reading. If you're constantly jumping between devices, this app could be for you. Monday.com is a project management app that helps you plan, organize, and track all your work in one visual tool.

8. **PASSWORDS.** If you're sick and tired of constantly struggling to remember passwords (and subsequently resetting them), you can use a system to keep track of them for you. As an example, LastPass remembers all your passwords and can be used across several devices. The program can store various passwords in your vault and audit them in order to help you create better, more secure passwords.

9. **WORK-REST.** The Time Out app is designed for easy break reminders, with flexible customization if you want it. It is very easy to fall into bad habits when using a computer for hours on end. You care about what you are doing, so you can sometimes push yourself too far or strain yourself. The human body isn't built to sit in one position for endless hours, gripping a mouse or typing on a keyboard. Time Out will gently remind you to take a break on a regular basis.

10. **HELP WITH WRITING.** Grammarly is a timesaving app to assist you with the effectiveness of your writing and the results you get with it. Grammarly automatically detects potential grammar, spelling, punctuation, word choice, and style mistakes in writing, as well as provides context-specific suggestions for wordiness, style, and plagiarism. It is available for your browser and also as an app for both iOS and Android.

11. **PHONE TRACKING.** The app, Moment, enables you to use your phone in a healthy way, giving you back time for the parts of your

life that matter the most. It allows you to see how much time you're spending or wasting on your phone on a daily basis and which apps you're engaged with the most.

12. **RECOVERY APPS.** The apps Headspace and Calm help with stress, sleep, focus, and anxiety and provide a variety of guided meditations, soundtracks, and videos. These apps can help you stay on track, perform better, and recover from your day.

GOING OLD SCHOOL: PEN AND PAPER

While technology and apps can be amazing tools for productivity and organization, I highly recommend using a notepad to write your three biggest items and to-do list. By writing on paper, I eliminate the distractions I might have come into contact with on my phone or computer—and I get the satisfaction of checking off things I do!

I also use Post-it Notes as visual reminders for important items. Whether I want to jot down my intentions for the day, my key focus items or an important reminder, Post-its are my go-to.

Time-Cleanse Your Phone

Our phones are an amazing tool to maximize our performance when used correctly and effectively. Cleansing your phone and setting it up to work *for* you, not against you, is one of the simplest and most powerful things you can do to transform your overall performance. As you learned back in Chapter 1, every touch, swipe, tap, click, and look costs you time. Here are tips to cleanse your phone so you can take control of your focus, attention, and time. *Use your phone for what you want, not have your phone use you.* As always, consider your lifestyle and business needs and adjust these suggestions accordingly as you cleanse your phone.

1. **CLEANSE YOUR HOME SCREEN.** Move all nonessential apps to a secondary screen. By making this small change, you eliminate the apps that may unconsciously suck up your time. Now, with a cleansed screen, you can mindfully make a choice about what you're using your phone for.

2. **TURN YOUR SCREEN TO GRAYSCALE.** To combat the charming and addictive nature of your phone, turning your phone to black and white instead of technicolor will make it less appealing and you will be less drawn to using it.

3. **REMOVE SOCIAL MEDIA APPS.** Delete Facebook, Twitter, LinkedIn, Snapchat, and any other social media apps. These apps are designed to constantly grab your attention. Removing them means you won't go on them!

4. **REMOVE E-MAIL APPS.** Constant connection to e-mail increases time pressure and anxiety. As discussed previously, have a predetermined strategy for how and when you check your e-mail.

5. **SHUT OFF ALL NOTIFICATIONS.** If a text message, e-mail, Facebook, or Instagram doesn't notify you every time something happens, you won't be looking at your phone. These alerts become nonstop distraction demons, and you need to get rid of them.

6. **REMOVE ALL UNUSED APPS.** Unused apps take up space on your phone and in your brain. Remove anything that is no longer enhancing your lifestyle, productivity, and performance.

7. **USE AN INSPIRING PICTURE OR QUOTE ON YOUR CLEANSED HOME SCREEN.** This will help train you to become present and reinforce your use of time every time you see it.

8. **PUT IT AWAY.** Practice working with your phone out of sight. Some research suggests that just seeing the phone can reduce your attention and learning by 10 percent.

9. **SET UP PHONE-FREE ZONES.** Create new rules for places you are not allowed to have your phone, such as in your bedroom or at the dinner table. Having phone-free zones allows and creates a connection with self and others and helps you reset and recover from the constant attachment to your phone.

10. **SET UP PHONE-FREE TIMES.** Schedule time during the day when you are free of your phone. Having periods of time without your phone or devices allows you to reset your focus, attention, and energy.

PERFORMANCE TOOLS

*Some people want it to happen, some wish it would
happen, others make it happen.*
—MICHAEL JORDAN

The following tools, tactics, and tips are focused on preparing your mind and body to perform at their highest level, as well as to recover and recharge to maintain consistency in your performance.

1. Get Enough Sleep

If there is one thing that has a global impact on your overall performance with your time, it is sleep. Sleep is considered the number one factor in creating and sustaining high performance. More than a third of American adults are not getting enough sleep on a regular basis, according to a new study published by the Centers for Disease Control.[5]

Lack of sleep can negatively impact decision making, reaction time, critical thinking, and memory function; reduce your immune function; and decrease your reservoir of cognitive and emotional resources from which you can draw to perform at your optimal level.

One study examined the effects of sleep duration and sleep debt. The results showed that with less sleep, people had higher perceived work pressure, multitasked more frequently, used social media more, and were more frequently in a negative mood.

Sleep is being recognized as such an important performance enhancer that professional sports teams across the board regularly have a sleep coach on staff.

In my coaching, I consistently find that clients who get the appropriate amount of sleep perform the best. I've also found that sleep is often one of the first things people sacrifice when under pressure to get everything done. The great thing about sleep is that it's something you can shift tonight, getting a good night of sleep and enjoying all the positive performance-enhancing benefits.

Here are some sleep tips to improve the quality and consistency of your sleep:

- Establish a regular bedtime/wake-up time.

- Remove your TV and any blue screen electronics (phone, tablet, etc.) from your bedroom.

- Maintain a dark, quiet, and cool (60–67° F) room.

- Do relaxation techniques—ritual meditation, breathing techniques, etc.—before bed.

- Invest in a good mattress and pillow.

- Journal a to-do list for the next day to get the list of items out of your head.

- Fill out the Complete the Day Worksheet from Chapter 9.

- Listen to the Time Cleanse Sleep track to improve your sleep. This track can be downloaded at www.timecleanse.com/book

2. Fuel Your Day

One key component in performance is the expansive topic of health and fitness. Similar to sleep, there are many resources on the topic, but one point that I can't drive home strongly enough is that fitness and nutrition matter. These two must-haves are key to maximizing your time, energy, and focus of each hour of your day. My message to you here is that your body biochemistry benefits in every way from being fit and healthy, and I urge you to take your fitness and health seriously and make them a vital part of your lifestyle in performing with time.

Find a program that suits your goals and intentions. I will share my personal go-to source, which is Venice Nutrition at www.venicenutrition .com, founded by Mark Macdonald, my personal nutritionist for nearly 20 years. Mark is a world-renowned expert and bestselling author in the field. There are many programs to fit your lifestyle. The key here is to find something that works for you, get started, and keep it up. This is one of the best areas for investing in and maximizing your Return on Time (ROT).

3. Take Coffee Naps

A quick coffee nap is an incredible way to boost energy and productivity during your day. This is a technique I learned from Dave Asprey, a researcher of human performance and founder of Bulletproof Coffee.[6] Asprey explains how it works and why:

> When you drink caffeine, it passes to your small intestine and gets absorbed into your bloodstream. It then kickstarts your brain chemistry and blocks receptors normally filled by similar energy transferring molecules of Adenosine, a chemical compound in your brain known for causing drowsiness. . . . When caffeine takes Adenosine's place in the receptors, it has the opposite effect: the nerve cells speed up giving us that jolt of caffeine energy and focus. So, what does any of that have to do with a 20-minute power nap? The brilliance of the coffee nap is that sleep naturally clears Adenosine from your brain!

Twenty minutes is the amount of time for the caffeine to fully kick in, so by the time you wake up from your nap, you're rested, recharged, and ready to go!

4. 4-7-8 Breathing

One of the best tools to instantly reduce stress and anxiety is breathing. How many times have you heard, "Take a deep breath," when facing a tense situation or when trying to clear your mind and relax? There's a reason: Consciously breathing causes a number of things to happen for us, from helping our minds relax momentarily to giving our bodies a break by introducing more oxygen into our bloodstreams.

Breathing, which is integral to our ability to be alive, is overlooked by most of us since we do it automatically. Yet if you think about it, each minute of our future is dependent on our next breath.

Dr. Andrew Weil, one of the leading wellness experts in the world and founder and director of the Arizona Center for Integrative Medicine, explains that each breath positively impacts our entire physiological system, from increasing our energy, to lowering our blood pressure, to improving our circulation and mitigating anxiety disorders without drug intervention.

One specific technique I teach to many of my clients is the 4-7-8 (relaxing breath) exercise that I learned from Dr. Weil.[7] These clients have reported a tremendous reduction in stress and anxiety, resulting in peace, clear-headedness, greater focus, and higher performance.

Follow the steps below for a quick way to reduce your anxiety, stress, and physical tension.

1. Sit up straight in a chair, close your eyes, and breathe gently. Let your body begin to relax.

2. Position the tip of your tongue against the ridge behind your upper front teeth. Keep your tongue in this position through the entire exercise, even when you're exhaling.

3. While keeping your mouth closed, inhale gently and fully through your nose while counting to 4 in your head.

4. Count to 7 while holding your breath.

5. Then, as you exhale through your mouth, slowly count to 8, making a whoosh sound.

6. Repeat Steps 3 through 5 two more times while keeping the same tempo of counts throughout.

To begin, practice this subtle but powerful exercise twice a day. Once you have the technique under your belt, you will be able to access it at any time. Use it before reacting when you are upset or triggered, and you'll perform at a higher level. It will help you respond rather than react. (*Note:* This is also a very powerful tool to help you fall asleep at bedtime.)

5. Head-Heart-Body

It's essential in today's fast-paced world that we make the right decisions to direct our time and energy to stay on course. A fast mindfulness technique I've adapted and added to is called head-heart-body, created by Pamela Weiss, a mindfulness educator.[8]

Follow the steps below to quickly get connected, centered, and moving forward mindfully with wisdom and intelligence:

1. Take one deep breath in (eyes open or closed) and then exhale, letting your body settle in and relax.

2. Bring your attention to your head and notice your thoughts. What are you picturing? What are you remembering? What are you reviewing?

   Just observe without judgment, and do not try to change your thought. You are simply working to notice your mental patterns.

3. Bring your attention down to your chest (or heart center) and take a deep breath in and then exhale. Notice your mood (feelings or emotions) now.

   Again, do not judge, shift, change, or alter anything. Just notice.

4. Now move your attention to your belly and take another deep breath in and out. Notice your belly rising and falling; then begin to scan your body and notice how it feels physically. Notice without any judgment and without fixing or changing anything.

5. Visualize your head, heart, and body connecting and communicating with each other. Ask yourself internally, "What do I need right now?" Notice whatever internal messages come forward, e.g., resting, having a meal, meditating, exercising, or focusing on a particular issue or topic in your business or personal life.

This evaluation can be done in as little as one minute for a quick check-in or longer if needed. By doing this head-heart-body technique, you will be better prepared to make mindful choices that support your performance.

6. The Circle of Excellence

The circle of excellence technique was developed by John Grinder, one of the founders of Neuro-Linguistic Programming.[9] This is a great tool to create a high-performance state so you can create massive results to start your day, big situations or events, or just to re-center yourself when you get off track. Here are the steps:

STEP 1. Remember a time when you were doing something extremely well. In the moment, you were confident, powerful, and successful. You felt unstoppable. Recall a specific memory, and if you can't connect with one, just imagine what it would be like to be unstoppable.

STEP 2. In your mind, draw a circle on the floor that's about three feet in diameter and about a foot in front of you. Make it large enough for you to step into. Now mentally place the memory into the circle on the floor.

STEP 3. Physically step into the circle you drew and into your memory. This is your circle of excellence. Let the energy flow from your feet to your head and flood your body with the positive thoughts and emotions of your memory. Let those feelings move through your entire body activating the feelings of confidence, power, and being unstoppable.

While in your memory, looking through your eyes, see what you see, hear what you hear, feel what you feel, and allow the sensations to come alive as if you're in it right now. You are now literally in that positive memory reliving it and anchoring to it.

STEP 4. As you feel the sensations and emotions of the memory peak, assign a color and symbol to associate with this state. This can be anything from a blue star to a silver arrow. By attaching a color and symbol, you now anchor this high-performance state in your nervous system to call upon at any time.

You can utilize the circle of excellence in situations where you feel pressured or stressed or where you want to prepare your body and mind to perform at your highest level at the beginning of your day, for a meeting or negotiation, or for anything of importance where you want to be at your best. Just call upon your anchor (color and symbol) and imagine that flowing through your body creating that high-performance state.

ENVIRONMENTAL CLEANSE FOR PERFORMANCE

As important as the Time Cleanse is for your time, so is the environment you live, work, and perform in. Your environment is a powerful force to maximize your time, focus, and productivity.

What You See

I love Marie Kondo's advice in her bestselling book, *The Life-Changing Magic of Tidying Up: The Japanese Art of Decluttering and Organizing*.[10] In her process, she asks readers when they are trying to decide what to do with an item, to ask one simple question: "Does this thing bring me joy?"

If it doesn't, remove it. Additional questions I ask include, "Does it have a practical or functional use in my life?" and "Is my environment organized, clean, inspiring, and motivating me to do my best work?"

Right now, look around in your home and at work. Are the objects and possessions surrounding you motivating and inspiring you for your greatest happiness and success? Or is your environment connecting you with memories and times that are no longer relevant?

Your environment influences your performance, so make sure you create one that supports your productivity and performance.

Things you can do to improve your visual environment: Get a whiteboard to list current ideas and projects, use Post-it Notes to remind you of your intentions for your day, surround yourself with special personal possessions that inspire you, etc.

What You Hear

What you hear has an impact on your performance and also affects your attention and concentration. Is your environment filled with music, conversations, or distracting noises?

Distractions of any kind can be a killer of your focus and performance. Noise especially can be detrimental. With the advent of open office space, data shows that employees waste 86 minutes every day because of sound distractions and interruptions happen about every 11 minutes.

A survey by the American Productivity & Quality Center found that 71 percent of employees think they would be more productive with additional space for individual work and quiet reflection.[11] Open work environments enable everyone to hear everything—colleagues talking to each other, phone conversations; even the tapping on a keyboard can make you crazy.

Each distraction due to an interruption, even a brief one, can cause you multiple minutes of lost productivity and time by dulling your concentration or by causing you to spend additional effort to reengage fully to return to where you left off. So if you don't or can't have a private workstation or office, investing in a good pair of noise-canceling headphones will work wonders. I use Bose, but there are plenty of brands to choose from, and even an old-fashioned set of earplugs will work just fine.

The table below shows the factors in your environment that either contribute to or contaminate your success.

CONTRIBUTE		CONTAMINATE
Organized, neat		Cluttered, messy
Cool temperature (68–72° F)		Hot temperature (73°+ F)
Quiet	Versus	Noisy
Positive visual cues		Visual distractions
Relevant items that surround you		Outdated items that surround you
Healthy food		Junk food

I challenge you to try at least one of the techniques from the "Contribute" list each day for the next week. If you do, you will watch your life, energy levels, happiness, and productivity transform.

You now have the most advanced tools and tactics in the world for identifying and cleansing time contaminants from your business and life and for supercharging your productivity and performance with your time. Remember, it is the planning that creates the environment of your success.

CHAPTER

11

Your New Relationship with Time

> Change the way you look at things and the things you
> look at change.
> —WAYNE DYER

YOU KNOW NOW THAT *YOU* ARE THE SOURCE OF TIME and the one responsible for it. No one can take this from you without your permission. It's all in your hands. It's 100 percent yours.

Through this book, you have reclaimed and found the most effective ways to reinvest your valuable time in what matters most. Moving forward, it's imperative that you continue to protect and perform with your time—and this chapter will teach you exactly how to do that.

The three Ms (Mindset, Map, and Mindfulness) have been covered individually throughout this book, and now that you are aware of all three, we will bring them together to collectively represent the approach that will change your relationship and performance with time forever in everything you do.

THE THREE Ms—THE THREE-STEP PROCESS TO IMPROVE QUALITY, EXPERIENCE, AND PERFORMANCE WITH TIME

Let's review the three Ms all together for the first time so you can put them into practice in your life:

1. **MINDSET.** You now know and understand that time comes from you and is abundant. You're also aware of the fact that you own it, are responsible for it, and can create as much of it as you need. By embracing and accepting this mindset, you will operate from a state that is free from time pressure and that allows you to be in your best mental, emotional, and physical state to perform.

2. **MAP.** Having a map directs you specifically to what's most important in your life, just like the GPS in your car directs you, reroutes you, and looks ahead for your best route. In order to master this step, you must have a specific success destination that is aligned with your purpose, values, and goals.

3. **MINDFULNESS.** Being fully present in the moment, where you are aware of your thoughts, your physical presence, your emotions, your senses, and all that is around you without judgment and with a sense of curiosity—which in the Time Cleanse process leads to improving the quality, experience, and performance with your time—Timefulness.

When these three steps are followed, you naturally reduce time pressure, enter a flow state, and become one with time. This is the ultimate way of living and being. Experiencing life to its fullest. Positive psychologist Mihály Csikszentmihalyi defines flow state in his book *Flow* as an "optimal state of consciousness where we feel our best and perform our best."[1] Being present involves "being completely involved in an activity for its own sake.... Time flies. Every action, movement, and thought follows inevitably from the previous one.... Your whole being is involved, and you're using your skills to the utmost," which creates your flow state of high performance.

That's what the three Ms can do for you.

Now that you're shifting to your new relationship with time and are investing it to your advantage, let me share with you what time is really about. Time is about one thing—creating memories that matter the most.

All you have is time, your most precious and valuable asset. While reaching your goals and achieving success is absolutely important, it's the memories along the way that make it all worth it.

Our memories are how we know who we are and what we stand for. That's why we're constantly sharing and reflecting on the positive experiences that give our lives meaning. They motivate, inspire, give us hope, and assist us in living fully as time passes.

Being relevant with your time is the key to those memories. Being relevant first starts with connecting with and embracing your unique gifts and talents that are aligned with your "why," your true purpose. This allows you to make a positive contribution with your time for yourself, your family, friends, colleagues, business, and the collective serving a cause greater than your own.

Being relevant is a shared experience. To me, life is about sharing and contributing in a meaningful way. Remember when something great happened in your life? After the experience of it, what did you do? You shared it with someone close to you—there was an abundance of positive emotions too great to keep to yourself. In the same way, that's what you're designed to do—share your gifts and talents with the world; that's when you experience your greatest connection, relevance, and meaning.

Immersing yourself in living your life from this place of relevance creates the ultimate, most meaningful memories. We find the greatest connection with experiences that best express who we are, involve what we most cherish, and engage us in what matters most in our lives.

Our level of engagement in any given moment (mindfulness) helps us to not miss the best moments. What are they? You already know the answer to that question. They are the moments you remember and live for.

It is only when we take the time to be present to what is really important to us that we can begin to create the memories that reveal, reflect, and remind us why we are here. We have a choice with our time and how we can consciously create memories that support the essence of who we are.

Memories become your legacy in the process of reaching your full potential.

LIVING YOUR LEGACY

Time = Memories = Legacy

> Did I Live?
> Did I Love?
> Did I Matter?
> —BRENDON BURCHARD

Each person has their own personal definition of what they desire their legacy to be, how they want to be remembered, and what contribution they will leave behind.

Many people focus on and think about their legacy toward the end of life. I invite you to see that it's an ongoing experience being created right now in every moment by what you do and say—it has been from your first breath. Throughout your life, each and every moment in time has the potential to contribute to your legacy.

Through the Time Cleanse process, you get to shape how you want to contribute and be remembered. It gives you clear direction about how to live your life right now in this very moment. Ultimately, it is how you invest your time that will create your legacy. Let's make it a great one for you.

With each of my corporate and individual clients, I ask them to complete a legacy worksheet. It's one of the most powerful exercises and experiences my clients go through. Now it's your turn to experience it.

Let's look at an example of this in action before you fill out your own worksheet.

STEVEN'S LEGACY WORKSHEET

How do I want to be remembered?

By my friends:
Caring, supportive, always in their corner no matter what, in good times and bad, there to the end.

By my spouse:
Supportive, protective, a leader, cherishing, patient, loving, kind and sweet, romantic, there to the end.

By my children:
Supportive, guiding, a leader, loving, a teacher, kind, there to the end.

By my parents:
That I lived a life of integrity, I gave more than I took, I loved.

By my colleagues:
Relentless, had grit, motivating, inspiring.

By God:
Was of service.

By the world:
Left it better than I found it.

By myself:
I left this world with an empty gas tank, left it all on the court with no regrets.

In the following blank worksheet, describe in each category how you would like to be remembered. If there are additional categories you'd like to consider, please add those as well.

Now try it for yourself.

YOUR LEGACY WORKSHEET

How do I want to be remembered?

By my friends:

By my spouse:

By my children:

By my parents:

By my colleagues:

By God:

By the world:

By myself:

Now that you have written out your answers, mindfully review each one and ask yourself, "Am I being that now? Is there room for improvement?" Without judgment and with curiosity, this can be a good check-in to make any adjustments in your life that you feel are needed in who you are being as an expression of your time.

This exercise is always an amazing eye-opener for those who go through it. For many, it's the first time they've declared how they want to be remembered, which translates to how we live right now. This exercise can bring up many different emotions, which is natural. Just let them flow through you, always connecting with the present moment and focusing on who you choose to be today that's representing your legacy. This is your time—you now know you own it, you control it, and it's time to make your move to create what you want with it.

AVOIDING LIFE'S MOST COMMON REGRETS

> Work for that feeling that you have
> accomplished something . . . Don't waste your time
> on this earth without making a mark.
> —JOE ROGAN

As you begin to consider your own legacy, you may want to know about the five biggest regrets people have at the end of their lives. Bronnie Ware, author of *Top Five Regrets of the Dying*,[2] was a nurse who cared for people at the end of their lives and discovered the following five main regrets, which can serve as a powerful reflection on your own life and legacy:

- I wish I'd had the courage to live a life true to myself, not what others expected of me.

- I wish I hadn't worked so hard.

- I wish I'd had the courage to express my feelings.

- I wish I had stayed in touch with my friends.

- I wish that I had let myself be happier.

The first regret, more than the others, really hits home for me: "*I wish I'd had the courage to live a life true to myself, not what others expected of me.*" That's because I see so many people being held back by their time toxins, limiting beliefs, environment, and distractions of today's world—wasting their lives and time on what someone else has programmed them to be and do.

This is the main reason I'm taking you through the Time Cleanse process: connecting you with *your* true purpose and what matters the most to you, so you don't have this regret.

The Time Cleanse provides the opportunity to eliminate these regrets right now in this very moment.

I want to share something that may be counterintuitive to what you may be thinking, a concept that was introduced to me by my friend and mentor Thom Knoles, a maharishi (master) of Vedic meditation. It's the gift of death: *We have an exact date and time on which we are born, and then when we die, we have an equally precise time stamp.*

Think about it: If you weren't going to die, you'd always have tomorrow. With that mindset, how motivated do you think you'd be? You probably wouldn't be reading this book right now.

The fact is that knowing you have a specific amount of time instinctively motivates you to get out of bed each day and make the most with the time you have. That time is your *life*.

Below is an exercise to get you in touch with potentially how much time you have left (it could be more or less than the average life expectancy of 78 years that we're using). I do this exercise in all my Time Cleanse events. It is one of the best processes to go through to motivate you to direct the time you have for what matters the most to you.

How Much Time Do I Have?

Step 1

> 78 years (average life expectancy) – your current age =
> # of years

Step 2

> (Step 1 answer) x 0.6 (to subtract sleep time) =
> # of years (your awake hours left)

Example (Ken, 45 years old)

Step 1

78 years – 45 years (current age) = 33 years

Step 2

33 years x 0.6 (to subtract sleep time) = 19.8 years
(Ken's awake hours left)

Now that you have your number, no matter what it is, you have an extraordinary opportunity: What are you going to do, and how can you make a difference and be relevant with the time you have left? At this point in the Time Cleanse process, you know what you want, you've cleared the toxins that have been holding you back or slowing you down, and you now have Timefulness tools to improve the quality, experience, and performance with your time.

LIVING LIFE THE WAY TOM DID

I always enjoyed getting a call from Tom Delaney, but the call I got in 2015 was different: "Big Steve, I want to let you know my wife, June, passed away." They were married for 50 years. He continued, "So I just wanted to let you know." I could hear the sorrow and loneliness in his voice as much as he tried to hide it. He then asked, "When are you coming to town?"

A few months later, I returned to Chicago around Thanksgiving. I was staying downtown.

Planning to visit Tom, I woke up the following morning and found eight inches of snow dumped on the city, and the streets were a mess. I wondered if I should reschedule seeing Tom for another time, but I decided to go ahead with the visit as planned and ordered a car to pick me up. After about an hour, the driver arrived and greeted me with warmth and a great smile. He warned me that the roads were pretty bad and the drive would likely take longer than expected. As time passed, I grew frustrated by the snow, I wondered if I'd ever get to see Tom that day. I considered just turning around and calling it a day, but I decided to take a few breaths to center myself, and I soon realized I was letting time pressure me. So I sat back and enjoyed the conversation with my driver until we arrived at Tom's.

When I got to his house, things were very different than they had been in the past. I opened the door, and there was an eerie silence. The Chihuahuas he loved were now gone. I wanted to ask about them, but I could sense it was now a different home, so I didn't. He yelled out "Big Steve" as I entered, and I found him sitting at the table wearing his white T-shirt, looking raw with his teeth out and a big smile on his face. There was coffee sitting there ready for us.

I sat down, and we picked up as usual. I told him about the Time Cleanse project I was working on and its principles and could see his interest. I could also see a request bubbling up in him as I talked more about it, "You know, Steven, all these years I was your coach supporting you, but now I need your help."

His request stopped me in my tracks. I said to myself, "He's never asked me anything like that before!" so I knew something profound was happening.

Tom said, "Here's the thing. Since my wife passed away, I'm kind of lost and time is dragging by day after day." He went on to ask, "What do I do now with my life?" and this big question hit me hard. Not just the magnitude of the question, but the pain and loneliness behind it. My mentor was asking me for advice, and I was both honored and taken aback by this. As I began to imagine what it was like to lose the love of your life and partner of 50 years and suddenly be alone, I let it all sink in.

After a few moments, I said to Tom, "You've got to fall back in love with something. I know it's tough, but that's what you have to do." He looked at me, paused, and stared off into the air. I felt the weight of the moment as he nodded in thought about what I had just said. Then he thanked me.

While nothing else was said as we moved onto another topic, I realized an interesting fact at that table. I was 51 years old, the exact age Tom was when I met him. All those years had passed, and I was now his age.

Times had changed so much. I looked up at the clock and realized that what seemed liked minutes had really been four hours and I had to go. I said to Tom, "It's time for me to go. I'm having dinner with my brother."

But as I stood up, he said, "Don't go, Steve. You just got here." And in that moment, 33 years flashed right before my eyes. It was 33 years since I met my rock-solid, loving mentor, and the man who was always in my corner, Tom Delaney.

I sat back down for what I intended to be a few more minutes because I just couldn't find it in my heart to leave quite yet.

A few hours later, I had to leave, but before I got up from the table, I looked him in the eyes. I once again told him how much his friendship and guidance meant to me and how it had shaped who I am today. I could see the tears streaming down his face as I spoke to him, and in that moment, I think we both deeply appreciated the friendship and love we had for each other. I stood up and gave him a big hug, and we said our goodbyes.

I opened the door to leave and felt the cold Chicago winter air hit my face. I looked back at Tom one more time as he smiled and waved.

That was the last time I saw Tom Delaney.

I got a call a couple of weeks later from his daughter, Tammy, who told me he had passed away. She explained, "He wanted me to call and let you know."

What I hadn't known was that when I last saw Tom, he was battling leukemia, and as he was going through treatment, he consequently came down with pneumonia. After my visit, his health declined, and he was taken to the hospital for more treatment. When he arrived, he told his immediate family that he was done with his treatment. He explained, "I've had an awesome life. I've done everything I wanted to do here on earth." He proceeded to tell his daughter he wanted her to bring the whole family here and tell "Big Steve" he was on his way, and then he said, "I've done everything I need to do in this life. It's now time to go back to see the love of my life." Tom passed away that night.

I share this story with you because our time is important. I had to make a decision that day either to combat the harsh Chicago winter to see one of my oldest friends or to reschedule and try to catch him the next time I would be in town. I made the decision that felt right in my heart and honored one of the most important relationships of my life, by not letting the weather deter me so I could give back to someone who had given so much to me.

If I hadn't been clear about what was important to me or had been distracted by other things that morning, I probably wouldn't have made that trip. I'm forever grateful that the lessons and techniques laid out in this book allowed me to make the decision I did and granted me the opportunity to see Tom one more time.

Here is how Tom was memorialized:

Thomas Joseph Delaney of Des Plaines; born in Ireland on September 13, 1931, he was a bus driver for Greyhound Bus Lines during his working years, he passed away in Park Ridge on December 18, 2015. He was preceded in death by his loving wife,

June. He is survived by his dear children Tammy Braithwaite and Thomas (Eileen) Delaney Jr. and his cherished grandchildren, Tanya, Kathleen and Thomas III. Family and friends will gather on Saturday, December 26 at 12:30 for a memorial visitation and a memorial service that begins at 2:30 pm at the Oehler Funeral Home 2099 Miner St., Des Plaines.[3]

The beautiful thing about creating a relationship with time through the Time Cleanse is that it makes your life, and every second of your life, more relevant. It provides you with more opportunities to connect with others, to make a positive impact, and to have a lasting legacy that you and your children and your children's children can be proud of.

- What will be said about you?

- Who will remember you and for what?

- What legacy will you leave?

The Time Cleanse allows you to get out of your head and get into relationships, projects, and endeavors that can change the lives of many people, not only your own. It gives you the amazing ability to stop at any moment and assess your priorities, cleanse yourself of anything not serving you, and *spend your time the way you really want—living a life worth living every moment of the day.*

The New Way of Living

Adding Life to Your Time and Time to Your Life

Fall seven times, get up eight.

—JAPANESE PROVERB

TIME INVESTED AND USED RIGHT, AS YOU NOW HAVE learned throughout the pages of this book, is the foundation for achieving lasting happiness and success. Through the Time Cleanse process, you have created a new relationship with time, where time is now your ally and supporter, allowing you to truly apply its benefits and full power to what matters most in your life. When your relationship with time supports you, anything is possible.

Time is the essence of life; it is everything you will do, get, or become—time is life itself. To have happiness and success and reach your full potential for achievement, simply put, you need to have time and know how to use time.

Research supports this philosophy in the sustained and effective use of time for reaching your goals and being a top performer in all fields.

Angela Duckworth is a noted researcher at the University of Pennsylvania and the author of *Grit*.[1] She studied top composers, doctors, spelling bee champions, West Point cadets, and other high-level performers to see what made the cream rise to the top. Her findings revealed that while talent and IQ are certainly factors in success, what's more important is the sustained application of effort (perseverance and passion) *over time* . . . What she calls "grit." Specifically, it's the ability to sustain effort over time in the face of adversity.

To break it down, perseverance and passion are absolutely essential to success, but without effective time performance, they only amount to wishful thinking and hope. Your success is determined by your ability to continually and consistently move forward with passion over time, without stopping, no matter what.

That's what the Time Cleanse is all about. It gives you back your time and shows you how to use it in the right way—to perform with it— increasing your capacity and ability to keep moving toward your dreams, desires, goals, and full potential. The Time Cleanse is the fuel for your passion, perseverance, and grit. It makes you grittier!

Once you know exactly what you want, and how time works, then everything changes. You get things done! What the Time Cleanse shows you is how to get that extra time needed to persevere, to be fully present in the moment by improving the quality, experience, and performance with your time.

It's hard to overestimate what an impact your new relationship and way of thinking and living with time can have on your life. Let me tell you a story about my mom that sums up my reason for sharing the Time Cleanse everywhere I go:

From the very beginning, I realized how hard my mom worked. She went back to work just five days after I was born, and she didn't stop working hard until she was in her seventies. On the other hand, my father left me and my mom soon after my first birthday, unceremoniously taking everything out of our house. He took the furniture, television, dishes, and even the towels. He even emptied the bank accounts—leaving us with just $3—all of which was discovered one evening when my mom returned home from work. We never saw or heard from him from that day forward. In that moment, she must have felt like her life had shattered into pieces. Yet with tremendous heartache and with no preparation, she picked those pieces up and pushed forward.

My mom was intelligent but never had the opportunity to go to college, a barrier I would watch haunt her throughout her whole career. She remarried several years after my father had left and was divorced a second time a few years later after my brother was born. Many times, she worked two jobs in order to support my brother and me, and every minute she wasn't at work, she was taking care of the two of us. She was in a constant struggle against time.

The early days were not easy. We were on and off food stamps and housing support. Through all of this, my mom did an amazing job given the circumstances. She was paid as an hourly worker making about 60 percent of what men did for the same job. It was painful to watch her work so hard to just keep us afloat. She never really had the time to enjoy herself or pursue her personal interests and dreams. We never seemed to get ahead, but she somehow always made ends meet. I never went without a meal or equipment I needed for sports, but I know it wasn't easy for her.

I am forever grateful for my mom's sacrifices and the lessons she taught me. Perseverance and the value of hard work were instilled in me at an early age just by watching her. She inspired me to have a positive attitude and taught me by example to never complain about what needed to be done. She taught me the importance of continuing to learn throughout life and of getting a college education. It was an honor to be the first one in our family to earn a college degree.

Even with all these lessons learned, one stands out to me more than any other, and that was her *grit*. My mom never gave up and always kept fighting; even in the toughest of times she kept moving forward.

And for that and so much more, thank you, Mom.

My mother is one of the main reasons my passion runs deep when it comes to time. I hate seeing anyone struggling with time, especially working moms, because it really hits home. But now I know it doesn't have to be that way. There is time for each of us to be great providers, parents, mentors, and leaders.

Your time is NOW.

I've developed an acronym for activation known as . . .

GRIT

G: GO FOR IT! It's your time right now to make your move. Make the right choices that will take you from where you are to where you want to be. Just like GPS in your car guiding your journey, when your thoughts, choices, and actions are aligned with your goals and big dreams, you've created a form of personal road map, a system to get you to your final destination in the shortest amount of time, with the fewest obstacles, all the while enjoying the ride.

R: RELEASE. Let go of your limiting beliefs, stare down your blind spots, and release your time toxins. Through your cleanse, you have released what is holding you back. As you shift into a state of high performance, it is time to let go of *all* the things that are no longer serving you. You are built for high performance, so release whatever is limiting you right now, and express your full potential. When you're living in your full potential, you can't help but move forward fast, building momentum and perseverance along the way.

I: IGNITE YOURSELF! Your *why* ignites and creates energy, inspiration, and motivation and ignites your passion. Stay connected with why you want to reach that goal and your vision of who you are becoming. It's the fuel for empowering your every move.

T: TIME. Take control of your time. It's the essence of life. Be the *boss.* There is only one boss of your life, and it's you. The only things you can fully control in this world are yourself and your time. Take responsibility for your life, your thoughts, your emotions, and your actions for every minute of every day. You are in control of your time, direction, momentum, and the speed at which you move forward. Own it. Every victory is yours. Take it. It's not about perfection; it's about progress and progressing. It's about taking the lead, learning from everything, growing every day, and filling your life with the full potential of *you* as you *continually add more time to your life and life to your time.*

Remember:

- You own time.

- You are fully present.

- You have 100 percent accountability for your time.

- You control the direction in which you are going.

The process of transformation has already begun, and your awakening has started. Awakening means this: Now you start your day with purpose, you set an intention, you have a clear sense of what you want from the day in a mindful way, and you do it. You are the source of time and in charge of it. Time is here to serve *you.*

You are not what you were before. Now you are activating your full potential. You focus on progress. Progress keeps you going. With each step and with each win, you get bigger and better results. You are connected with your purpose, making a difference in a relevant way for you and the collective. Your time is now!

My mentor and coach Tom Delaney was always in my corner. Through all the highs and lows, he was always there, coaching, supporting, and cheering me on. As you complete this book and take on what matters most in your business and life, I want you to know that I'm in your corner with the power of the Time Cleanse supporting you every step of the way no matter what!

Understanding and investing in your life through *time* will reward you immensely, take you beyond your biggest dreams, and enrich your life every day. By living and performing with *time* as your greatest resource, you can now stay focused on living your true purpose, making great memories along the way, and building a legacy you're proud of.

Ultimately, the Time Cleanse gives you the freedom to be all that you are and all that you are meant to be. Your time is finally yours again.

Remember:

There is only one time, and it's *now*.
There is only one direction, and it's *forward*.

NOTES

Chapter 1

1. Social & Demographic Trends, "Life's Priorities: Time Over Money," Pew Research Center, November 5, 2010, www.pewsocialtrends.org/2008/04/09/inside-the-middle-class-bad-times-hit-the-good-life/480-3/.
2. Shawn Achor, *The Happiness Advantage* (New York: Currency, 2010).
3. Martin Seligman, *Learned Optimism: How to Change Your Mind and Your Life* (New York: Vintage Books, 2006).
4. Maarten W. Bos and Amy J.C. Cuddy. "iPosture: The Size of Electronic Consumer Devices Affects Our Behavior," Harvard Business School Working Paper, No. 13-097, May 2013, https://www.hbs.edu/faculty/Pages/item.aspx?num=44857.
5. https://www.elitedaily.com/news/world/study-people-check-cell-phones-minutes-150-times-day and https://www.nytimes.com/2017/01/09/well/live/hooked-on-our-smartphones.html.
6. Tristan Harris, "Our Society Is Being Hijacked by Technology," Center for Humane Technology, http://humanetech.com/problem/.
7. Courtney Ackerman, "The 23 Amazing Health Benefits of Mindfulness for Body and Brain," Positive Psychology Program, March 6, 2017, https://positivepsychologyprogram.com/benefits-of-mindfulness/.

Chapter 2

1. Amy Morin, "Your Failure to Differentiate Stress from Pressure Could Be Your Downfall," *Forbes*, March 18, 2015, www.forbes.com/sites/amymorin/2015/03/18/your-failure-to-differentiate-stress-from-pressure-could-be-your-downfall/#6d25ae793a32.
2. Case Western Reserve University, "Perception of Time Pressure Impairs Performance," ScienceDaily, February 16, 2009, www.sciencedaily.com/releases/2009/02/090210162035.htm.
3. Peter R. Brown, Wendy J. Brown, and Jennifer R. Powers (2001), "Time Pressure, Satisfaction with Leisure, and Health Among Australian Women," *Annals of Leisure Research*, 4:1, 1-16, January 14, 2013, 10.1080/11745398.2001.10600888.
4. Friedman and Rosenman. Association of a Specific Overt Behavior Pattern with Increases in Blood Cholesterol, Blood Clotting Time, Incidence of Arcus Senilis and Clinical Coronary Artery Disease, *JAMA*, 1959, 169:1286-96.
5. Gay Hendricks, *The Big Leap: Conquer Your Hidden Fear and Take Life to the Next Level* (New York: HarperOne, 2009).

Chapter 3

1. Simon Sinek, *Start with Why: How Great Leaders Inspire Everyone to Take Action* (New York: Penguin Group, 2009), 37-40.
2. Peter Gollwitzer and Veronika Brandstatter, "Implementation Intentions and Effective Goal Pursuit," *Journal of Personality and Social Psychology* 73, no. 1 (1997).
3. Mary Morrissey, "The Power of Writing Down Your Goals and Dreams," HuffPost, September 14, 2016, www.huffingtonpost.com/marymorrissey/the-power-of -writing-down_b_12002348.html.

Chapter 4

1. Helen O'Neill, "Scientist's Death Helped Increase Knowledge of Mercury Poisoning," *Los Angeles Times*, September 14, 1997.
2. Napoleon Hill, *Outwitting the Devil: The Secret to Freedom and Success* (New York: Sterling Publishing, 2011).

Chapter 6

1. Ashley V. Whillans, Elizabeth W. Dunn, Paul Smeets, Rene Bekkers, and Michael I. Norton, "Buying Time Promotes Happiness," PNAS, August 8, 2017.
2. David Goggins, *Can't Hurt Me: Master Your Mind and Defy the Odds* (Lioncrest Publishing, 2014).

Chapter 8

1. Brené Brown, *Dare to Lead: Brave Work. Tough Conversations. Whole Hearts* (New York: Random House, 2018).

Chapter 9

1. Daniel Pink, *When: The Scientific Secrets of Perfect Timing* (New York: Riverhead Books, 2018), 26-35.
2. Brad Stulberg, "The Scientific Way to Harness Timing for Peak Mental and Physical Performance," Medium, February 9, 2018, https://medium.com/personal-growth/ the-scientific-way-to-harness-timing-for-peak-mental-and-physical-performance -8ceb30703942.
3. Mel Robbins, *The 5 Second Rule: Transform Your Life, Work, and Confidence with Everyday Courage* (Tennessee: Savio Republic, 2017).
4. William McRaven, *Make Your Bed: Little Things That Can Change Your Life…And Maybe the World* (New York: Grand Central Publishing, 2017), 3-9.
5. Eisenhower, "Introducing the Eisenhower Matrix," https://www.eisenhower.me/ eisenhower-matrix/.
6. Christian Voelkers, "Benefits of a Standing Desk," VersaDesk, February 20, 2018, https://blog.versadesk.com/index.php/2018/02/20/benefits-standing-desk/.
7. J.D. Meier, *Getting Results the Agile Way: A Personal Results System for Work and Life* (Washington [Bellevue]: Innovation Playhouse, 2010).

Chapter 10

1. Chris Bailey, *Hyperfocus: How to Be More Productive in a World of Distraction* (New York: Viking, 2018), 63-65.
2. Gloria Mark, Daniela Gudith, and Ulrich Klocke, "The Cost of Interrupted Work: More Speed and Stress," Conference on Human Factors in Computing Systems, January 2008, https://www.ics.uci.edu/~gmark/chi08-mark.pdf.
3. Kathrine Jebsen Moore, "How E-mail Harms Your Intelligence," Priority Management NSW and ACT, www.prioritymanagement.com/nsw/resources/resource.php?resource_id=53.
4. Adam Gorlick, "Media Multitaskers Pay Mental Price, Stanford Study Shows," Stanford News, August 24, 2009, https://news.stanford.edu/2009/08/24/multitask-research-study-082409/.
5. CDC, "1 in 3 Adults Don't Get Enough Sleep," Centers for Disease Control and Prevention, February 18, 2016, www.cdc.gov/media/releases/2016/p0215-enough-sleep.html.
6. Dave Asprey, "Opposites DO Attract: Coffee Naps, the Bulletproof Power Nap, Explained," Bulletproof (blog), May 18, 2015, https://blog.bulletproof.com/coffee-naps-bulletproof-power-nap/.
7. Andrew Weil, "Three Breathing Exercises and Techniques," Andrew Weil, M.D., www.drweil.com/health-wellness/body-mind-spirit/stress-anxiety/breathing-three-exercises/.
8. Pamela Weiss, "Guided Meditations," Appropriate Response, www.appropriateresponse.com/teachings/.
9. "Circle of Excellence for Powerful States," NLP Mentor, https://nlp-mentor.com/circle-of-excellence/.
10. Marie Kondo, *The Life-Changing Magic of Tidying Up: The Japanese Art of Decluttering and Organizing* (New York: Ten Speed Press, 2014).
11. Krista Krumina, "26 Office Improvements from A to Z to Boost Your Team's Productivity," DeskTime, April 10, 2017, https://desktime.com/blog/26-office-improvements-from-a-to-z-to-boost-your-teams-productivity.

Chapter 11

1. Mihály Csikszentmihalyi, *Flow: The Psychology of Optimal Experience* (New York: HarperCollins, 2009).
2. Bronnie Ware, "Regrets of the Dying," Bronnie Ware, https://bronnieware.com/blog/regrets-of-the-dying/.
3. https://www.legacy.com/obituaries/name/thomas-delaney-obituary?pid=176967224.

Conclusion

1. Angela Duckworth, Christopher Peterson, Michael D. Matthews, and Dennis R. Kelly, "Grit: Perseverance and Passion for Long-Term Goals," *Journal of Personality and Social Psychology*, Vol. 92, no. 6 (2007): 1087-1101.

Index

About the Author

STEVEN GRIFFITH IS A NATIONALLY RECOGNIZED author, speaker, researcher, and performance expert. He is considered one of the leading authorities on the connection between time, productivity, and performance. For over 25 years, Steven has been helping the world's most successful executives, CEOs, entrepreneurs, military leaders, professional athletes, celebrities, and organizations around the world discover their true potential and perform at peak levels.

He provides a strategic and effective approach to changing our relationship to time, allowing organizations and individuals to close performance gaps and realize their full potential. Based on thousands of client engagements over two decades, Griffith's Time Cleanse is the first solution in the world that both "adds time to your life and life to your time both in your business and in your life."

His clients have included the *Jimmy Kimmel Live!* talk show, United States Military, Citibank, Wells Fargo, Los Angeles Police Department, and players and coaches from the NBA, MLB, NFL, and NHL.

Born and raised in Chicago, Steven is a former Golden Gloves boxer and Illinois state heavyweight champion.